y Steven Elliott Borodkin

guin Books

York

-7

be reproduced in any form or by any electronic or mechanical
tion storage and retrieval systems, without written
or, except for the use of brief quotations in a book review.

STREET L

STEVEN ELLIOT

Street Level

Copyright © 2025

All rights reserved.

Published by Red Pe

Bellerose Village, Nev

ISBN

Digital 978-1-63777-73

Print 978-1-63777-737-

No part of this book may
means, including informa
permission from the auth

"You begin to think you are the home of evil, darkness and most of all sin.

You think if anyone could see the truth about you, they would be repelled, recoiling from you as if from a poisonous snake. You think if what is true about you were revealed to you, you would be struck with horror so intense that you would rush to death by your own hand.

Living on after seeing this being impossible."

Helen Schucman,
A Course on Miracles

Dearest Zack,

You have seen in your time on this planet, through struggle and determination, what took me seventy years to discover. Showing me that each day deserves a smile. That nothing is unattainable if you simply put your mind to it.

Thank you for your light and your love, my darling son. Without you, this book would have no end. With you, life is immeasurably more beautiful.

Love,
Dad

To My First Editor,

Smart, intuitive, open, honest. A beautiful soul. You heard my voice and saw my artistic eye. You believed in me, then you gently pulled and prodded. Showing me how much more I had to give of myself to others, through this mosaic of stories and ponderings. Together we've created something special to share with the world.

Always,
The Author

Dearest Deb,

Thank you for your love, tolerance, and seeing me. Without you this would never have been possible. There are no words to express my deep love for all you are.

CONTENTS

Foreword — xi

BOOK ONE
STREET LEVEL

The King and the Lower East Side — 3
Summer, 1968

Birthdays, Bats, and Circumstance — 6
Bayside, Queens - August, 1964

The Beating of Jimmy Fingers — 8
August, 1968

The James Dean of Mulberry Street — 12
1968

Do Not Call Me Junior — 16
1968

Cousin Bobby — 19
1968

Flying Lessons — 25
November, 1968

Blow Jobs and Bakeries — 28
August 10, 1969 - My Fifteenth Birthday

Wall Street and the Dancing Chickens of Chinatown — 32
1969

Landlords and Junkies — 36
December, One Week Before New Year's 1969

Jack Abramowitz — 42
Spring, 1970

An Odd and Violent Abstract Design — 50
September, 1970

BOOK TWO
DRAMATIS PERSONAE

Wellcome to Book Two 55

MOTHER

Contemplating Death, Kodachrome, and Phone Books 61
1961

Cake and Nicotine 62
1962

Clowns in the Closet 68
1964

Alice Being Alice - PART I 70
Alice Being Alice - PART II 73

FATHER

Eighty-Eight Keys and the Marlboro Man 77
1962

Little Boat, Big Ocean 80
1964

Trumpets, Icons, and Flying Saucers 82
1970

The Nazis, Freight Trains, and Split Melons 86
Summer, 1973

Jewish Cowboys 89
1989

Death, Dirt, and Good-Byes 91
1998

GRANDPA MOE

Old Spice and Pop-Tarts Summer 99
Summer, 1962

The White Whale and the Bar Mitzvah Boy 104
November, 1966

Driver of the Chosen People 107
November, 1972

Unintended Good-Byes, Pancakes, and Glycerin
Tablets 112
1974

GRANDPA ABE

Love and the Creative Mind   119
1961

Stage Left   123
Friday Night, January 17, 1964

The Weight   127
1979

BOOK THREE
BLOOD, GOD, ANGELS, AND DOGS

Three Little Assholes   131
September, 1974

Ghosts and Zombies   135
September, 1974

Slipping into Darkness   138
November, 1974

Tino Takes a Dive and Cha-Cha's Last Dance   141
Xuan Loc – January 1975

Members Only   145
Kennedy Airport – February, 1975

A Cage Full of Ghosts   147
July, 1975

Saint Derrick   151
November, 1975

Praise the Lord and Pass the Biscuits   154
November 1975

The Story of Christmas, Laoni, Angel   158
Canada - December, 1975

Billy Comes Home   166
Spring, 1979

Farther North   169
Spring, 1979

Timid the Dog   172
Fall, 1979

BOOK FOUR
THE ROAD HOME

A Soft and Solid Space   179
1980

Terra Firma   180
1980

The Girl on the E Train   187
1984

A Life Given, A Life Taken   189
September, 1988

Afterword   201
About the Author   203

FOREWORD

My life, as most of us, is defined by the experiences and traumas we endured as children. I've shared some of mine with family and friends over the years. Some, until now, had never been exposed. Out of shame and fear of sharing the places I'd been and the things I'd done, and what was done to me.

At times building one lie upon the next, not understanding why I was lying at all. Out of shame, continually for decades the pain and weight of my lies and untruths to hide these experiences and abuses from others became overpowering then devastating. It affected everything and everyone I touched for a long time. It has been a long and rutted road to get to who I am.

The act of rape is more than physical. For the giver, as they place their noose around your soul and pull, their pride swells. For them, their behavior represents a failure to be able to command the notice they crave through normal channels. Thus, the perpetrator of this heinous physical invasion is emboldened by their posture *and dominance over their victims in the act itself. For me, the physical act became insignificant after the first time.*

It is the scar the noose left in its soiled wake that has lasted a lifetime . . .

"Stevie, come here, it's time for your bath."

The Author

BOOK ONE
STREET LEVEL

1968

Doctor Martin Luther King and Bobby Kennedy get assassinated in that same year. Completing a trifecta of political assassinations that took five years to achieve.

Ten-thousand miles away, on the other side of the world, the North Vietnamese carried out the spring Tet Offensive, trying to slaughter as many Americans and South Vietnamese as possible and take control of Saigon. A task they'd finally complete on April 30, 1975.

THE KING AND THE LOWER EAST SIDE

SUMMER, 1968

The Lower East Side of Manhattan back in the late 1960s at its lowest level was divided into kingdoms. The stoops of the tenement buildings its thrones. The higher up you sat on the scarred and trampled stoop of your building, in some ways, the more of a made-man you were. You were a king. You received all kinds of cool shit. Free cigarettes and weed. If you were lucky enough to have a working girl on your turf, you got free pussy if you were old enough to care. As king, you could also get a bit off the top from whatever went down on your turf. That was, if you knew about it. There were so many people making so many deals and running so many frauds, it was hard to keep track most times. Somehow, we all got along.

Two things on the street were never tolerated. It either got you hurt or dead. You did business in your space and, without exception, *never* spoke against or about anyone that you did business with. If you stayed cool, you could really get over without getting in each other's way. If you were lucky enough, you ended up with enough dough to treat yourself to a small bag of primo weed and a plate of matzo brie with a cup of hot chocolate at Ratner's, a huge dairy restaurant that served the best breakfast below Saint Marks Place. It was located on Delancey Street at the foot of the Williamsburg Bridge on the westbound side.

How did you get to be a king? I had no idea and really did not give a flying fuck. I had much bigger issues to contend with as a fourteen-year-old runaway. Being the king and getting free pussy and weed was the furthest thing from my mind. At the present time, not being part of any group and being the new kid on the block, and for a very brief time fresh meat, I was at the bottom of the food chain. Street level for now was off limits if I wanted to stay physically intact and keep whatever cash I had. To my way of thinking, the only way around this world of bullshit every day was cutting across the tenement rooftops five stories above the ground. I was tired of sneaking around my own neighborhood and even more tired of paying to get my ass kicked. I loved the idea of cutting out whole blocks of bullshit just by staying aloft. Jumping from building to building thrilled me. I fell in love with it. The freedom of cheating death rocked me to my core.

The stench of shit and garbage was too heavy to make it that high off the cement and asphalt below. Hundreds of feet above it all, the air was cleaner. Free to breathe. As I passed over each building, there were large pigeon coops housing dozens of well-fed birds. The cooing and muffled sound of their voices a soundtrack to my weightlessness. The men and boys who tended these coops would collect, feed, and train these birds. Releasing them, letting the flock circle overhead, leading them from the roof tops with long thin rods that they circled over their heads. Orchestrating the flock skillfully, and with a bit of luck, drawing pigeons from competing flocks from other rooftops to their own, lured by the alpha males. It was a peaceful and unencumbered world. Apart from the minutia and war zone below. These pigeons had names, like Bomber, Grey Baby, Blue Bell, Fly Boy, and Night Sky. The men who tended the birds would stop and watch me jump in calculated strides, bursting from one building to the next, flying, mocking their birds, landing feet first most times on the next building. I fell in love with the freedom of flight. As if I was

Icarus. Reckless and defiant of all limitations, holding myself aloft through the two feet of air between each building. They'd wave to me with those *what the fuck* looks in their eyes. Sometimes I would stop, out of breath and bravery, peering over the side. My halted breath an acknowledgement of my immigrant status in this urban, alien, landscape. Staring down on streets teeming with life below, I sometimes thought when I finally do slip and fall, plummeting head first onto the pavement, I would be just another lost soul. Dead and pushed aside. My corpse left orphaned in the absence of my spirit as it slips away into the crowded, derelict humanity of my new neighborhood. I slipped one day as I launched myself through the air, just making it to the next building. Sitting on the opposite roof, cuts on my hands from a hard landing, with small pieces of broken bottles and dirt now embedded in the palms of my hand, my back up against the very wall I almost missed. Shaking, bleeding, I peed my pants. Coming to the realization that I *would* die from this subconscious, suicidal propensity. So, it seemed, like everyone else, the only way to get any approbation on the streets was to be a part of the machine that was the streets. I surmised that I was either going to be grease or gear. I chose gear. It was either that or go back to that fucking animal...my mother.

I sat there thinking about the repeated rapes and beatings that I had endured at her hands before I finally ran away. The unbearable shame of all of it coursed through my body; I was septic with the idea of pain as a tool, and I was done running. I had left home to save myself, not kill myself jumping tenement roofs. My anger of not wanting to be fucked over or touched anymore finally had fermented into a beautifully physical manifestation. Then something inside spoke to me; it kept repeating in my mind, blocking any other thoughts from penetrating. It said, *Fuck them all, Stevie, fuck them all to hell.* I listened intently. The stench of my own piss drying in my pants, the pain in my palms starting to throb was intoxicating. I fuckin' loved it. Violent retribution was on the menu and was best served cold.

BIRTHDAYS, BATS, AND CIRCUMSTANCE
BAYSIDE, QUEENS - AUGUST, 1964

On my tenth birthday, I received a kid-sized baseball bat from my dad. The bat were one of those stand-out gifts that you never forget...

Wearing a wrinkled, stained white dress shirt, dirty day-old boxers and socks, my dad stood there. In a cloud of Marlboro and depression. His failure spilled off of him. The moment reeked of lack of communicating his commitment as my father. Even at my age with my own hidden pain, my heart broke for him because I knew how much he loved me. How much we loved each other and all the things we were scared to tell.

Calling the bat Wonder Boy, he told me about a book he had read, *The Natural*. He explained that he named my new bat after Roy Hobbs' magic bat. The bat that made Roy Hobbs a star (as well as Robert Redford in the movie) once again after such a tragic stop to his life at such an early age. Pulling another fresh Marlboro out of the pack, lighting it, pausing in recollection, he continued. The smell of lighter fluid and the poison smoke he sucked into his lungs momentarily making me hold my breath. Breathing out the brown fog from his lungs as he smoked, "You go and do the things that matter to you,

Stevie. No matter what life happens to throw at you, do it all. Swing away, don't be afraid of what they throw at you. Go for the fence, go for the gold. Again, inhaling the smoke. Now seemingly exhausted, blowing out smoke and air like a deflating tire, slumped over, turning his back to me, walking away. (Decades later I read the book after seeing the movie with Robert Redford playing Roy Hobbs.)

I sat there stunned, brought to a stupor of silence, holding the bat in my left hand with my right hand gripping the side of the bed, white knuckled. Numbed by the definable realization of what he had just said to me. I saw his gift, not as the bat it actually was, but a message of freedom and power, empathy and immediate understanding that he would never have the opportunity to do all the things he wanted to do, but that I still did. Maybe his blank awareness of something strange, not right, between me and my mother. A feeling that he knew that something was wrong, couldn't figure out, and was afraid to ask.

The bat gave me real pleasure. Its effect was surprisingly instantaneous. Its reality came from the feeling of its purpose in my hands. My bat-Excalibur. It felt my pain and frustration. It melded together wood and flesh, in intention, power, and destruction. I was afraid of its spell over me. I placed it under my bed, then finally in my bedroom closet, afraid it would roll out from under the bed one day on its own and ask me to pick it up. Four years later, one summer morning I ran away. I grabbed it first before anything else I packed. I took my toothbrush, clean socks, underwear, and that little fucking bat.

But I digress...

Now four years later, almost to the day at this moment, as I sat on the roof in my pee-stained jeans, I plotted the unabashed and violent debut onto the streets of my new neighborhood. The following morning the little bat's destiny was not going to be about connecting with any baseball in any ballpark. Batter up, mother fucker.

THE BEATING OF JIMMY FINGERS
AUGUST, 1968

The Sunday morning air had already come to a boil. The heat of another summer day lifting itself off the streets, carrying shimmering waves of well-fed flies with it. The smell of dog shit, human waste, piss, and garbage coated everything. The feeling of despair and the hopeless recognition of another day sticking and then peeling off the bricks of the overcrowded tenements like chips of lead paint.

Jimmy Fingers and his crew covered the stoop like someone's dirty laundry. Their turf ran right past my front door, directly across the street from where I was staying at my cousin Bobby's flat at 109 Eldridge Street. (We'll get to my cousin Bobby in a bit.)

There he sat, the king, red hair, sweaty, in his black cut off T-shirt on the top step, cigarette bobbing up and down from the corner of his mouth as he barked out what he said. The king, like a potted plant, sitting on his throne of cracked cement. Jimmy ran all the bullshit and business up and down Eldridge Street, south two blocks to Hester Street, then north two blocks to Rivington. Jimmy Fingers, as he was called, lived with his folks, first generation Irish immigrants, on Rivington Street. He was a big guy for sixteen years old, with green eyes and a mean streak that made his face twist into what Jimmy thought of as a tough guy look. To me it looked like he was suffering from some type of head trauma. He got his nickname by breaking the fingers of the people who owed him money for small-time bullshit. If you didn't pay . . . crack. *Everyone* who did business on the streets had their own way of evening things out . . . breaking fingers was Jimmy's.

Pinky, appropriately named, was a small, soft, washed-out toothpick of a kid who looked like a hairless little rat. Costumed in too-big dirty jeans, black Chuck Taylors, and a white cut-off T-shirt, he was the first one to notice my structured, mellow advance as I crossed the street in the group's direction. I was wearing a denim jacket in ninety-degree heat, with my bat-Excalibur underneath, white T-shirt, the same pee-stained jeans, and my new work boots. Using the pounding of my heart, keeping my fear and my anger just below the surface, I marked time counting my steps and staying focused on the task ahead. I was so very tired of jumping roofs and being hassled, touched, or pushed around, always having these guys, and everyone else, take whatever money I dared to take outside with me. Disgust and pain from my mother's beatings and rapes echoed in my head, I was immersed in pain and looking forward to sharing it in full with the group of dirtbags directly ahead of me, now nonchalantly beginning to notice me.

I placed my left hand on the bat, deepening my grip on the base of this little piece of wood, in a zone of sorts. As Pinky fully rose to his feet to my oncoming assault, I walked up to him and kicked him hard in the balls with the tip of my new work boots. I watched as his little pink body folded in two, hands between his legs, collapsing on the sidewalk in front of the stoop knees first, then on all fours, trying to recover, howling in pain. This gave me more joy than I could remember feeling at the time, and at that moment, unbelievable power. Walking around his crumpled body, I stepped up to Jimmy and pulled out Wonder Boy. In one slow-motion and poetically fluid roundhouse, I swung and came across hard. The bat had just fulfilled its destiny. *He swings, he connects, what a hit.*

The sound of the bat against the left side of Jimmy's head was a sweet, muffled *THA-WACK*. It seemed to echo endlessly down the street. Knocking him completely off the stoop, first sideways into the railing, then tumbling forward off his throne to the gum-stained sidewalk, hitting his head on the way down, landing on his back. The sound was out of place amongst the ritual clatter and constant static at 9:00 in the morning. Its audio presence summoning those who wanted to look, and everyone did. It scattered the pools of flies and roaches eating breakfast on the tops of the stuffed, gray steel garbage cans that lined the front of the buildings. The bat split Jimmy's head with its tip, connecting with the top left side right above Jimmy's ear. I am surprised it didn't kill him, which was my goal. Over and over, the bat came down hard on his back, stomach, and legs. He covered his head with his arms. His cries of pain, the real smell of his fear, and the sight of his blood bathed me in what I knew was gloriously wrong. It was sweet and alien, warm, way too inviting, and horrific. It was, in the end, both beautiful and satisfying. Standing over him, my legs spread, his prone and bruised body lay under my control. It felt deliciously wrong. Adrenaline coursing through my body, I stared down at him and stammered out the words, *Ya ddddon't look like mmmuch of a tttough ggguy now, do you, aaaaasswipe?*

Through his bloodied mask, he gurgled back, "You're a dead man, mother fucker."

I continued looking down at him. I had willingly become lost in the surprisingly joyful rage and scale of my violence. I knew, for Jimmy, his reign as king was over, and in that momentarily gold medal moment, I raised the bat over my head and like Moses holding the ten commandments, I commanded, not "Let my people go." Instead I bellowed out, *Go fffffuck ya-ya-yourselfff, JJJJimmy*. He laid there, a small pool of blood leaking from his ear and mouth, motionless. Fuck you, Jimmy; Fuck you, Mom . . . fuck everyone, I don't need them or anyone else. Not anymore. But as they say, karma is a bitch.

Jimmy's guys, those who hadn't helped Pinky back up and run off, now over the shock and brutality of Pinky's and Jimmy's beatings, not wanting to be embarrassed in front of the neighborhood, who had all come out to watch by this time, had placed themselves in my way, leaving me no retreat but through them. Keeping a tight hold of my bat, letting it fall to my side, swinging it back and forth in my left hand, a small drop of Jimmy's blood staining its diameter. I made my exit as calmly as my body would allow and pushed through them, then the crowd, back onto the street; I had no issue with these guys. I walked away. My adrenalin was at a fever pitch, and I was scared shitless.

The first punch to my kidneys brought me to my knees. I had never felt such pain. The moans in the air were mine this time. They blocked the sky with their fists and feet. Lying on my side curled into a fetal position, I covered my face with my arms and hands. The bat was ripped away from me as I went down. Grateful they were too stupid to use it on me after witnessing the enormous success I had with it on their "king." I had been through much worse and more invasive interactions in my young life already. So, just like Jimmy Fingers, that red-haired piece of shit, I laid there, arms covering my head, waiting for his gangs retribution to end. It wasn't even close to what my mother had done to me.

THE JAMES DEAN OF MULBERRY STREET

1968

I heard some guy yelling in the background, *Hey! Enough, enough, stop, stop, step-the-fuck-back!* The beating was over. He had a tough-guy voice and when he came into view, a good-guy smile. His body cast a shadow over my currently prone and pain-laden position on the pavement.

"Hey, kid, you alright? Jesus." He bent down, extending his right hand to help me to my feet, whispering in my ear the first of many secrets still untold between us. "Excellent work with Jimmy. He was a big pain in my ass, too many people with broken fingers. Cops just took him to Bellevue Hospital up on 1st Avenue for stitches and a concussion." The next time we saw Jimmy, two weeks later, he had a limp and stitches over his left ear. He crossed the street every time he saw me. Part of me felt almost diseased in a sense for the way I beat him, by the way he was broken, the way I had broken him . . . No gang, no throne, and no fingers to break anymore. King my ass.

We stood in the silence that only the aftermath of violence can elicit, then, as a matter of simply stating a fact, Junior continued, "You're good, ya know what I mean, kid? No one's gonna fuck with you no more, you're good. Do you understand who I am around here and what you just did?"

Helping me brush myself off, he offered me a clean white handkerchief out of his back pocket to wipe the blood off my face. Handing me my bat back, he leaned in close again and said, "Nice bat, kid. Fuck, look at your face; they beat you good." I knew they had, I hurt all over.

Spitting blood out of my mouth and checking for missing teeth, "They didn't beat me good enough; they didn't fuckin' kill me."

Ignoring my blood and my stupidity, he went on, "My name's Tony. They call me Junior cause my dad's Senior." And in the same breath he added, "You like pizza?"

Dominic's Pizzeria smelled of warm baked dough, tomato sauce, and grease. In a booth of worn red vinyl cushions, we sat facing each other for the first time, separated by a narrow wood table covered with a small vertical aluminum napkin holder, salt and pepper shakers, a container of grated garlic, and a used but clean ashtray. All grouped together in the center space at the end of the table against the wall.

We felt an immediate connection as we sat in momentary silence, decompressing from what just happened, waiting for the pizza slices to be placed on the table, the silence enough to ensure that I didn't remember either of us ordering.

Perfect rows of framed, autographed photos of the owner Dominic with Frank Sinatra, Dean Martin, Pat Cooper, and other less famous, but equally important, Italian celebrities of the day were hung on the wall opposite from where we sat. Outside, under a green- and red-striped awning, the front window was open onto Mott Street and turned into an outdoor counter. There were small groups of people talking, eating pizza, and drinking cold bottles of Coca-Cola, finding an oasis under the awning's shade.

Tony spoke first, "They would have killed you for what you done to Jimmy in front of everybody . . . good thing I was passing by. You just claimed the top step . . . is that what you wanted, cause it's yours now . . . are you hearing me, wise guy?"

Listening to every word, I answered through sips of iced Coca-Cola from a waxed paper cup that was magically placed in front of me with a wave of Tony's hand when the food was delivered. The cold waxed paper felt good against my swelling lips. My words came out in a deep, swollen sigh. Smiling, I looked up at my benefactor . . . no one had ever called me a wise guy, not that way.

"Fuck, man," tears stinging my eyes, "I hear you . . . I got tired of taking the roofs to get around, that's all . . . Is the top step really mine?"

Tony's eyes widened a bit then relaxed again, "You're the new kid jumping roofs? We heard about you, you crazy son of a bitch. That takes both balls and brains . . ." He continued, "How fucking old are you kid?"

"Fourteen, just this August."

He took the last bite of his pizza, smiling now, and continued. I could see, he was a little impressed. "Pick up your bat, wipe the blood off, put it back in your jacket, and finish your pizza, kid." I gingerly placed the last of my slices into my mouth, trying not to bite my swollen lips in the process. It was at that moment the most outstanding pizza I had ever tasted. Watching me, shaking his head in disbelief like he had discovered something new, laughing, still chewing his pizza, he swallowed and lit a Newport. "What's your name anyway, kid?"

Swallowing, sniffling, feeling a bit better, I answered, "My name is Stevie; I live with my cousin Bobby over on Eldridge Street."

Without missing a beat, he said, "I know your cousin. He's that fuckin' junkie that lives on the fourth floor over at 109 Eldridge. He's your cousin? Well, fuck me . . . Let's go before the cops come back and ask questions and see your face. They'll know who you are soon enough, trust me. You'll be a big deal for a little while."

When we walked into Dominic's and sat down together a half

hour before, I noticed the nods and the way people looked at us. As we got up to leave, Dominic came around from behind the counter and said, "Thank you, guys." He held the door open, and we strolled out without paying a dime. "Tell Senior I send my best."

DO NOT CALL ME JUNIOR
1968

Senior, allegedly, was one of the most well-connected guys to one of the largest families up and down the East Coast in Little Italy. Tony, Senior's only son, took care of the streets on the north side of Canal Street from West Broadway east to where Canal Street ended at the foot of the Manhattan bridge, then north to the corner of Bowery and Delancey. He managed the bookies and running numbers, dice games, and card games, racking in major cash for his efforts and handing it all off to his father who, in turn, kicked twenty percent back to his son who, in turn, would hand me and Larry the Bean a nice juicy cut. Remember, this was 1968; that type of cash would have been astronomical to anyone. Imagine being a fourteen-year-old runaway. These assorted enterprises alone took in well over three-hundred-thousand dollars a month. You do the math. They owned the streets, and I got to unglamorously walk in their shadow. Selling protection to all the shop owners and landlords from all the scumbags for a small fee, of course. That was handled and collected by Senior's bodyguard and driver, Fat Jerry. (We'll get back to talking about one of my dearest and most trusted friends down the road. I loved that man.)

Most importantly, Tony provided 24/7 security for the working girls in his father's territory. They received, all twenty of them, nothing but the best food, housing, and clothing. Of course for them, protection was free. They, alone, were responsible for over one-hundred-eighty-thousand dollars a month in cash. We used to feed it into the machines to count it. Senior made us wear gloves because he said it was, "dirty money." Those twenty young ladies got well compensated. Senior paid them and paid well. He knew as a businessman they and their clientele were a never-ending and major source of income. His girls were clean as a whistle and drug free, except weed.

Tony knew the streets. He was as sharp as the blade he carried in his front right pocket. Charismatic, dangerous, good with math, he always commanded respect just by being present. A twenty-one-year-old good looking, perfect height of six feet, all cast in a frame of understated muscle. His hair was jet black, slicked back hard, and combed in a ducktail. He smelled of wise-guy cologne and cigarettes. Always dressed as an up-and-coming wise guy should be dressed. European knit custom-made shirts, black custom-tailored slacks, and impeccably polished Italian loafers. He kept a fresh Newport behind his right ear and a snub-nose .38 under his belt in the back of his pants, behind his tailor-made sports jacket. Junior was the epitome of cool, the perfect cliché.

I helped him run numbers and make cash pickups and deliveries of weed all over the Lower East Side during the day. Hitting all his father's dice games, card games, and whorehouses at night, then collecting at the end of each night.

Together we walked the streets with our friend Larry the Bean (because his head was shaped like a Lima bean).

The three of us ate in different restaurants and walked out without ever looking back or even leaving a tip. I knew every bookie, scammer, dirt bag, working girl, and con man that he did business with. They knew me, as well, and also knew I was connected.

Tony was authentic. Tony was a tough guy, and the real fuckin' deal. He did not like being called Junior, so I never called him that. I liked having my face intact.

He was my best friend and mentor. In all the years I knew him, he never pulled his weapon.

He was the James Dean of Mulberry Street.

COUSIN BOBBY
1968

Bobby was a likable junkie with long, matted brown hair tied back in a half-ass ponytail, bad breath, and a fourth-floor, one-bedroom, cold-water flat on the Lower East Side of Manhattan. He also was the twenty-year-old son of my dad's first cousin. Bobby had avoided the draft by going to college. Conforming to his father's well-planned future at the time seemed like a suitable alternative to getting killed in a war ten-thousand miles away.

During the second semester of his junior year, they busted him using the science lab to cook up his own LSD, selling it to students and faculty. Expelled, he left home. Following the drugs, drawn to the Lower East Side of New York, he got himself a job delivering weed for a local dealer. He moved into a two-bedroom flat for sixty-five dollars a month. Until he discovered heroin.

JUNE, 1968

One day after summer school, I threw my books in a trash can and boarded a Q169 bus to Jamaica, Queens, then at 169th Street and Jamaica Avenue transferred to the F train to the Lower East Side of

Manhattan, emerging onto the south west corner of Delancey and Essex Streets. Like a fledgling, I was momentarily blinded by fear of the unknown, this new blistering reality and a piercing light that seemed to be everywhere. Humanity in abundance and color cascaded all around me, through me, never even seeing me. This place, a gathering of languages and cultures, and an intense smell that was too much for the space it had, tumbling, spilling over into the streets. All seemingly laced together in the most extraordinary dance I had ever seen.

I had spent months gazing as my eyes glazed over as I looked for this place. Never realizing how far south it was. The MTA subway map my dad kept in the kitchen drawer finally gave up my destination after months of finding time to sneak a look when no one was around so they wouldn't ask what I was up to. Nevertheless, there it was at the bottom of Manhattan, the East River one mile east, directly beyond the FDR Drive revealing itself under my father's penciled circles around his various business appointments in the city. Hello, Delancey Street. I was familiar with the subway, taking it almost every weekend with my hero, Grandpa Moe, to Radio City Music Hall when I was only single digits, maybe just ten years old. (Grandpa Moe, another story, another adventure.)

I reached into the pocket of my Levi's and grabbed the one dime I had taken for this purpose. I dropped it in the slot and slowly dialed my parents from a badly-injured phone booth outside the Essex Street Market. I remember to this day the receiver smelling like vomit. Hoping my parents' answering machine turned on. Then my mother's voice, "Hello, you have reached Howard and Alice Borodkin, please leave a message at the beep, and we will be sure to get back to you." Beeeeep...

"Mom, Dad, it's Stevie. I'm spending the summer with Cousin Bobby in the city. I'll call you, he doesn't have a phone. I'll be fine." Click. I made my way toward Bobby's neck of the woods. I had heard my father talking about him on the phone and remembered the name of the street he lived on. It had a cool sound to it... Eldridge

Street. Everyone knew who Bobby was. It was apparent from the get-go everyone knew who everyone was down here. I walked into his building forty-five minutes later and climbed the steps to the fourth floor, taking in the squalid surroundings. Having second thoughts, I knocked on the door. Seconds ticked by, sedated by the gloom, giving me the opportunity to take in the smell...

"Who's there?"

"Cousin Bobby? It's Stevie... Howard Borodkin's son."

The door opened. He let me in, "Hey kid, make yourself comfortable."

With no questions asked, he got it. It had to be big.

SEPTEMBER, 1968

After using Jimmy's head as a baseball, I had actually gone on and survived a mind-blowing three months living in this inconceivable, alternate universe. Catapulting myself from a totally dysfunctional working class Jewish family and a sexually abusive mother. Battered, deeply and emotionally bruised, I had landed here by my own choosing. Now, a junior assassin with a Little League bat, pockets full of money, food, clothes, and best of all, protected by being part of a crew of a certain ethnicity who occupied and ran a certain neighborhood just one block west of Bowery for about ten square blocks, and beyond (if you get the drift). Trust me, the best was yet to come... so, I shall continue.

I called my parents every weekend, knowing there was a better chance of my father answering. "Hey, Dad," trying to stay calm and sound even happy. But my anxiety manifested itself into what I affectionately named the death chill from hell. This happened every time I called home. The sensation can best be described as being pulled apart from the inside by blocks of ice-shaped fingers. The pain would start to pulse in the center my groin and the back of my neck simultaneously, then come together and collaborate to bring me down by using my spine as a conduit. The reaction similar to the

Titanic hitting the iceberg that brought her down. The intense stress and anxiety of self-induced subzero pain made me shake uncontrollably all over and gasp for air, making my toes curl in my work boots and my eyes water, gripping the receiver so tight my hand hurt for minutes afterward as I held it away from me so my father wouldn't hear my struggle. Debilitating.

I paused, then blurted out, "I've decided to stay with Cousin Bobby, and I'll be going to school here in the city." A silence you could almost hear ensued. My father's breath rolled in and out through his nose as he, wheezing, inhaled deeply on his cigarette, its sound far away, almost like a different universe . . . I waited. Tick, tick, tick . . . still hoping for hope. I placed a nickel on the shelf under the phone to add three minutes if my time ran out before he decided to reply. Why couldn't I say, "Come and get me, Dad"? Was he waiting for me to ask? Was that *my* responsibility? In retrospect, some sixty-five years later (if that is even possible), maybe I stayed still in that moment not wanting to go back home.

It took unbelievable power riveted and held in place by palpable feelings of shame and true worthlessness for what was repeatedly done to me that somehow it was all my fault. I bore the burden, not wanting to bring my disgusting and unimaginable pain, my hell, to the rest of my family. Feeling most protective over my father. From what? From whom? Was I seeing him as a victim of my abuse as well. Deep shit for sure.

Finally, he spoke, "I am, we are, extremely disappointed, Stevie. Your mother and I are very angry and terribly upset; no one understands what the hell this is all about." I knew she was standing there listening, that fucking monster. *I should have killed that bitch* kept rolling through my mind as my father's voice became muted behind the deliciously dark and dangerous thoughts filling my head. Living in this comforting yet ultra-violent landscape, walking around with a bat under my jacket didn't help much. Then, the final blow from my own father. Dismissively, he went on, "I'm sure you think you have your reasons, but what could be that bad, really, Stevie? You're a kid!" I could imagine him looking up from his chair and winking at my mother for her approval. My mother shaking her head up and down in a good-job kind of way.

"You'll miss home soon enough and want to come back once school starts again." What the fuck did that mean? That weak-ass crap cut deep and hurt in an untouchable place for most of my life. Inflection points are never painless, hence the word, point.

If only he would have said, "You stay right there, kiddo. I'm coming to get you. I love you. You are my only son; you mean the world to me, Stevie. Hang on, my love. I'm on the way."

I would have relented. I would have gone back, "Yes, Dad, please come and take me away from this place. I want to come home. I'm coming home, Dad; come and get me. I love you so much." I would have told him every detail. I want to believe he wanted to say it but didn't know how. So odd, in fact, it was so fucking tragic. Instead, what he so horribly conveyed, not even understanding the depth of what he had done, gave me permission to carry on with what I was doing, and what I was becoming . . . a sexually-abused Jewish fourteen-year-old kid who ran away from home and jumped rooftops now for just shits and giggles, who didn't give a fuck about anyone but the small circle of trusted older men he was with. Was no more than a misplaced soul who carried a bat around under his ever-present jean jacket like some weird, sacred pacifier and who beat his pain into everyone who angered him and wore his mother's face. The world could go fuck itself. I was done with it. So be it.

Cousin Bobby put needle after needle in his arms, thighs, and between his toes and fingers. He would disappear, coming back days later, looking like death. I watched him fuck whores, buy and sell dope, get high, and make promises he could never keep. I'd catch him on top of our kitchen table, knowing he never cleaned it, sloppily fucking away to beat the band. His junkie friends, dirty apparitions of men and women, sad leftovers from yesterday's lunch, dragging themselves in and out of our flat. Some not much older than me. Sitting in a circle on the floor in the front room, I'd watch them shoot up and draw the blood from their arms back up into the syringe so others could inject the mix of blood and heroin into their own bodies. They got high, fell out, woke up, fucked, and left. The flat smelled of sex and vomit. At times, it was so intolerable, I slept at Senior's club on a cot in the back, surrounded by cases of beer, boxes of stolen electronics, and bags of cash. Still, it was safer than going home to her, so much safer . . .

FLYING LESSONS
NOVEMBER, 1968

Bobby got beat to death across the street from our building by two guys using metal pipes. Tony and I had just come from Dominic's. We saw the crowd, then heard what was going on. I remember someone yelling, "They're gonna kill him!" Yet not one person tried to stop it. I was watching Cousin Bobby's end. I felt the weight of the pipe each time it landed on my cousin's face or skull. Smack, crack, whack, over and over. I pushed forward; I could feel the melding of power as an ever-agitated bat-Excalibur vibrated under my denim jacket. Ready to pound my own pain and beatings out of my mind by inflicting pain and death onto others. I had never used the bat again since Jimmy, but I was on the cusp of another mistake. I knew it, too, but didn't give a fuck. It was time to establish it and my presence once again. I tensed, coiled, ready...

The bat's voice howled in my head, *What the fuck, Stevie? Save Bobby. Why are you just standing there? He saved you, now go save him.* The voice, my own, the same dark, angry voice that had spoken to me as I lay locked in the hallway closet in the home I had so desperately escaped from, remembering lying there sore and scared after my mother's rapes and beatings. Planning all the inglorious ways I could murder my own mother. Then once again up on the roof, smelling from my own urine as I plotted Jimmy's end. The voice screamed in my head, bleaching out the reality of the consequence, telling me, *It would take just two goods swings. We'll kill them both, smash their junkie fuckin' brains in and be done with it . . . heroes! . . . You'd be accepted and loved by everyone . . . Isn't that what you wanted anyway? To be loved by everybody, no matter how much of a worthless piece of shit you are and how ashamed of yourself you are? Then God-damn-it, Stevie, swing the fuck away. Swing, swing, swing!!*

Tony felt my body coil as my left hand reached under my jacket. He held me with his arms wrapped around my chest, his head pressed hard up against my shoulders, the bristle of his whiskers and hard, gelled hair scraping against the side of my face. I fought against his grip, not understanding why he was stopping me. The constant voice in my head droning on. Now at a high volume, animated, fever pitch. It screamed at me, *Swing away now, smash their junkie heads to pieces.*

Love for my cousin pushed tears from my eyes as the man that saved my life kept talking into my ear, "Stevie, listen to me. It wouldn't look good for me or Senior if you or me got hurt or hurt anyone else in front of all these people trying to stop three junkies from killing each other." I felt the conflict, pain, and anger in Tony's words. "Junkies get killed, Stevie, cause they lead fucked up lives. Bobby was just another junkie, family or not. You fuckin' hear me, kid? Let it go, I told you once before I got your back, so don't worry."

In a vise-like grip against my passionate defiance, gentle and calm as a summer breeze, he whispered with the same intensity, "You get what I'm sayin? We are family. I love you, let it go."

Through my tears, angry and confused, bat-Excalibur and I in a hybrid voice replied, "Yeah, I fuckin' get it." And in that insistent and almost overpowering condemnation as the screaming voice in my head reluctantly conceded to Tony's will, fading, fading . . . *You coward, you fucking stupid, ungrateful coward, coward, coward,* fading. In an adrenalin trance, I gave in. "Yeah, fuck you, Tony. I get it, now let me go." Tony squeezed me once more in recognition and dropped his arms to his side, then pulled the Newport from behind his ear and lit it. It was over. For now, anyway. Nothing ever really ended out here on the street.

What seemed like hours had taken only minutes. It ended as Bobby slumped, then crumbled to the ground, his face unrecognizable. Small pools of blood, seemingly framing the mess that was once his face. His two attackers ran off, leaving the pipes, curious faces of people with nothing else to do but look at the carnage and Bobby's body lying on the sidewalk. The ambulance arrived minutes later. The driver and his assistant scraped my cousin's remains off the street, wrapped his broken, faceless body in a blanket, then unceremoniously dropped his remains on a stretcher. Putting him into the back of the ambulance, the siren faded uptown. The crowd thinned, people giving the scene one last glance over their shoulders, then going about their business shaking their heads.

The two junkies who beat my cousin to death had disappeared. Nobody had seen them for days, so I had thought. When I asked Tony a week later if anyone had seen the guys who killed my cousin, he replied, "Didn't I tell you not to worry? We found them, everyone saw them. Jerry and I picked them up and took 'em to Prince Street for flying lessons."

Good-bye garbage. Off the roof and into the alley, I presume. They could have gone up there to get high, slipped, and fell. What was I saying, anyway?

BLOW JOBS AND BAKERIES
AUGUST 10, 1969 - MY FIFTEENTH BIRTHDAY

Sunday morning, I was sitting in Fat Jerry's Buick before I took off to Queens to see my family for my surprise birthday dinner. Me and Fat Jerry had developed the comfort of just sitting together without saying a word, watching the street, enjoying each other's company, listening to hits from the 1950s on WCBS-FM.

Jerry broke the silence. "I'll make ya a deal kid, I'll pay the girls to get ya tubes cleaned for your birf-day down on Cherry Street if ya take me to Mr. Lee's bakery for some breakfast. It can, ya know . . . be a gift from me ta you. Who don't want their dick sucked for the first time on a Sunday morning for their birthday?"

"Who said this would be the first time, Jerry?"

"Come on, Stevie, who ya talkin to?" Continuing, "Besides, if I go to the bakery myself, Senior will know I was there."

Senior was on Jerry's fat ass to stop eating. He was Senior's driver and personal bodyguard when Senior left the club to go anywhere. He had gotten so enormous that he could barely fit behind the wheel of his new Buick that Senior had bought for him, let alone appear threatening when asking anyone for money, enforcing the rules, or protecting his boss. I imagine.

Chinatown had their own bakeries, full of row after row of warm sweet rolls and hot roast pork buns, ten-cent black coffee, and rich, dark, black tea. I knew all the best ones. All were owned by my friend, Mr. Lee.

Thinking over his offer, I replied with caution, "I'll take ya to the bakery. But I ain't bustin' my nut the first time with no strangers, Jerry. My first blow job should be from one of Tony's girls, right?"

Pinching my check with his fat and deadly fingers, "Okay, Stevie, you got a deal. Just don't tell Senior about the bakery."

We shook on it, then he turned the car south into Chinatown.

Jerry cruised across Canal Street. Anyone that knew what was going on out on the streets recognized the sable-brown Buick and Senior's driver. I directed the big man to one of Mr. Lee's bigger bakeries at the end of Eldridge and East Broadway under the Manhattan Bridge knowing Mr. Lee would be there.

"Wait here, Jerry. I'll be right out."

Three minutes later, in the front seat next to the big man, I had a 20-dollar tip in my pocket for my birthday from Mr. Lee, two very large black coffees, one dozen assorted fresh pastries, piping hot in a white cardboard bakery box and tied with a thin blue cord, and an envelope with five thousand dollars for Senior in my front pant pocket. His cut from the opium and whores for that past week, I imagine. I never looked in the envelope, so it could have been a letter of some kind or other type of personal correspondence.

Mr. Lee looked out the window of his bakery and saw Jerry sitting in the car. He would now mention he saw Stevie and Jerry last Sunday picking up pastries and coffee, along with the envelope. Senior knew about Jerry's visits to his different food haunts, without me or anyone else ever mentioning a word to him. But I told Senior anyway, before Mr. Lee did. I felt bad giving up Jerry, given our deal and what I was getting out of it. No matter how insignificant you thought it was, it was not cool to ever keep *anything* from Senior.

The smell in the car was an unfair and overwhelming distraction for the big man.

"Jerry, keep your fuckin' eyes on the road. Let's not get pulled over." We left Chinatown, and Jerry drove us to Cherry Street and the FDR Drive. This was the spot where the girls were allowed to work the street. Right off the Grand Street exit, going south off the FDR. Easy on and easy off, if you will. No pun intended.

The Buick pulled over and stopped. I jumped into the back seat. I knew the drill, from what everyone else had told me. Jerry rolled down the front window on the curb side. One of the girls sauntered over.

"Hey, baby, I'm Katie, what kinda action ya looking for, guys? Again?! You were here two days ago, Jerry! Hey . . . who's the kid? He's cute."

"Katie, meet Stevie. He needs your attention."

"A new fish? . . . Sure thing."

Katie was young, brunette, and simply adorable. Not yet carrying the stains and scars of her profession on her face and in her eyes. She got into the back seat next to me smiled, kissed me on the cheek, told me to relax, wished me a happy birthday, put my hands on her tits, and then unzipped my fly, sticking her hand inside my pants, rummaging around like she was looking for loose change in her pocketbook, until she found what she was looking for. Up front, Fat Jerry was picking bits of pork and pastry dough out of his teeth with a toothpick, as he finished off the box of goodies, drinking his second container of coffee. I was enjoying Fat Jerry's gift big time in the back seat. Feeling like one of those pictures in my magazines and not believing this was happening. For the first time, feeling like a man. And hoping I could see Katie again and not in the back seat of Fat Jerry's Buick.

Katie came to my flat once every couple of weeks for the next five months. For most of that winter, we spent our nights smoking weed and having sex, eating Chinese takeout, drinking cheap wine, and having more sex. I was fifteen years old, she was twenty-four.

It snowed hard the last night Katie would ever come over. The kitchen window was open to control the amount of steam heat. A small pile of snow had blown in and started to accumulate on the windowsill, melting slowly. Dripping down the wall, leaving a trail, making a hissing noise as the drops of water hit the top of the radiator and evaporated. The sounds of the city, muffled by the snow, coming through the open window. Our clothing laid mixed together on the floor by the side of my bed; it was cold outside. Small puddles of water had accumulated around our boots and shoes by my front door from running out to get our stash of hot and sour soup and steamed dumplings. We made love under piles of blankets and quilts by candle and streetlight.

After, lying back against the pillows in my bed, I was spent. I watched Katie get dressed. Panties, T-shirt, sweater . . . then, finally, her jeans. In the scattered light running through my flat, she was a study in film noir. Feminine and poised. Her sex and beauty oozed from the pores of her skin. In the infant stages of my manhood, I was overwhelmed at that moment. It was slow-motion and so extremely hot. A movement in female grace. It was my first man-moment.

I rose off the bed, naked, reached for her, but at the last minute, my dresser drawer, and pulled out my money, hoping it didn't cheapen her mood the way it had just cheapened mine.

"Here, Katie, take this. Consider it a loan."

"No, baby boy, this is too much." She put on her coat and slipped the eight twenty-dollar bills into its left pocket.

"You ever need anything . . . anything at all, you ask me, Katie. I'll always have your back. Do you hear me?"

The declaration of my promise to her echoing back to me. Frugal in the absence of her reply. My cock was flat. My head hurt. I needed a shower to scrub off the regret. I wanted to get really fuckin' high and, maybe, sleep forever.

The snow by the open window now sat piled three inches on the outside sill. The storm got worse. I never saw her again and didn't touch another woman for three years. Instead, I elected to propel myself into the abyss. Dragging anyone else who wanted to test their own existence.

WALL STREET AND THE DANCING CHICKENS OF CHINATOWN

1969

It had been almost a year since my arrival and violent entrance onto the streets of the Lower East Side. Tony had taught me well, and I knew what I was doing, for the most part. With respect, I made my way. Making friends and money. Knowing that someone had my back as long as I did everything out of respect for what was given to me, and to the people, who's gift it was. I learned very quickly where my source of joy and abundance sprang from. I honored and nurtured the hell out of its existence with the deepest respect.

Tony was the man without exception ten blocks in every direction. From where we all sat, our crew, on our stoop in front of my building, we were all kings now. We bought and sold whatever came our way. Everything did. Stereo systems, boxes of new sneakers, cameras, winter coats, cigarettes, and weed. Always weed.

After Tony checked to make sure everything was on the square, we would turn all the merchandise directly over to Senior for a cut. It was a safe and sweet existence. Whatever we touched turned to gold. We were invulnerable.

For the right price, we took you to the best opium dens Chinatown had to offer. We collected twice, once from the mark and once for the delivery of said mark to our benefactor and friend, Mr. Lee, on the south side of Canal Street. It was easy to spot these Wall Street guys walking aimlessly up and down the street in their two-thousand-dollar Armani suits. Thinking that taking off their ties would make them look unassuming, only making it more obvious to all of us.

Tony always started the conversation, "Hey, whass up? Follow me. I know what you want." Then immediately handing them off to me or Larry the Bean, sitting across the street, to walk them across Canal Street to the Land of Oz. They would gaze down at us, seeing the streets in our eyes. It scared the shit out of them. It thrilled them. With a glazed look of anticipation, they vicariously lived in our shoes for just that instant. Experiencing the violent, degenerate thrill of our freedom.

We delivered dozens of men to Mr. Lee's opium dens that summer. He paid us five bucks each time we delivered someone. The mark paid us ten. We were rolling. When Mr. Lee did well, Senior did well, and so it goes.

Mr. Lee was an exceptionally big deal in Chinatown and also my good friend. I learned quickly to show him respect and honor every time I was in his presence. He liked the idea of a big mouth Jewish kid working for his friends in Little Italy.

He was a long-time business partner and trusted friend of Senior. He stood at just five feet, four inches tall, one hundred and forty-five pounds. He had piercing, dark brown eyes behind the thick, black glasses he wore. Always dressing in traditional Chinese garb. A shrewd businessman. He had come through Ellis Island with his family some fifty years before. Like most new immigrants to this country, he saw these streets paved with gold.

When the Lee family left China, they took whatever belongings they could carry. Mr. Lee's father had seen years ago that money was easy to make but hard to keep. Catering to human weakness was a universal service and always profitable. Drugs and whores seemed the simplest way. The Lees simply expanded on the business they had back home with more freedom in America to pursue their dreams.

His businesses included bakeries, gambling parlors, whorehouses, and a small collection of opium dens. These multi-roomed, low ceiling flops were located off Pell and Mott Streets. They were littered with sofas and cots, past their date of expiration, covering their scars and holes with blankets and dirty throw pillows. Makeshift beds for the Wall Street crowd and candlelit caves in the basements of restaurants. The smell of the food and pedestrian traffic was a perfect cover for the pungent, hot, and bitter smell of the drug and the two-thousand-dollar suits that staggered in and out. Young, tired, stoned, half-naked Asian girls would escort you to your cot or couch, making you comfortable only to place a long thin pipe in your mouth, lighting it for you with a longer thin candle, as you took deep breaths, inhaling the smoke. Then as you zone out, showing you just enough tit and ass, with a brush of their hand across your crotch, getting you hard as a friggin' rock before you check out to dreamland. Assuring them a much bigger tip when you checked back in fifty minutes, when they gave you a happy ending. I never did opium or got jerked off, although I was offered their undeniable releases repeatedly. It seems like such a waste of time.

Old school Chinatown on the south side of Canal Street was the smell of fresh fish and old fish. Rooms filled with mahjong, dice, and card games behind the faux walls of restaurant kitchens. Bakery shelves lined with fresh baked pork buns; steamed vegetable dumplings served in bamboo pots on a bed of cabbage leaves. Cheap whores, really amazing dope, and the pitifully famous dancing chickens of Chinatown.

The dancing chickens were live birds, placed in wire cages, then into small four-sided glass booths, framed and mounted on a wood base. These brightly-painted yellow and red booths were chained up outside of the game arcades and tourist traps selling cheap imitations of Chinese pottery, furniture, and toys for the kids that were sprinkled all around Chinatown. Meant to draw the tourists in when they saw others of their kind standing around the booth, watching the unfortunate thing perform its inevitable dance of death. When you dropped a quarter in the slot, it would unleash a small but effective current of electricity that would make the bird jump around until the animal, or your time, was used up. I never knew what made the unfortunate thing jump around, then lay on its side. I thought it was resting. I was so oblivious to the pain of others and never gave it much thought.

LANDLORDS AND JUNKIES

DECEMBER, ONE WEEK BEFORE NEW YEAR'S 1969

Thanks to Senior, Cousin Bobby's flat was now mine for the same sixty-five dollars a month that he had paid. Which didn't matter, because Senior always gave me the cash to pay my rent. It was his way of expressing his thanks to me for keeping eyes on Mrs. Facetti and helping her with her day-to-day chores.

Mrs. Facetti was the building's landlady. Rent free and landlord for life. She and Big Ray, her twenty-four-pound cat, occupied the ground floor apartment, with a small garden in the back, where she grew tomatoes and assorted herbs while Big Ray sat under her aluminum beach chair in the shade watching them grow.

Senior did business with the owner of our building. In one way or another, he did business with the owners of most buildings in our neighborhood, allegedly supplying them with protection against other families. But I would have no idea what you were talking about, if you were ever to ask me what I knew, about something I never mentioned. Rumors, always rumors.

The Facetti family came through Ellis Island in 1911. Angeline was thirteen years old. Now, at seventy-one, she was the sole survivor, having lost two sisters, one older, one younger, a brother who was killed in World War II, and a husband who, after fifty-one years of marriage, passed away five years earlier back in 1964. She had two sons and five grandchildren who all lived uptown above 14th Street. She became a very dear woman and a mother to all of us: a mother to me. I had grown to love her strength and clarity, age, and presence. Mrs. Facetti, who was forever dressed in black, never lost her patience or her Italian accent.

Mornings I'd take the steps two at a time to the ground floor. Always opening the door into Mrs. Facetti's apartment. Knocking softly and walking in. Scooping Big Ray up in my arms, smothering him in kisses, burying my face in his fur. He smelled like old rugs and oregano. Always warm and dusty from sleeping under the heater or some underside of furniture in some corner in their apartment. As was habit, I'd place him down, only to pour a bowl of milk for him and a glass of milk for me. Treating myself to a slice of fresh ricotta cheesecake sitting on the immaculately clean kitchen counter on a transparent, rippled glass plate.

"Stevie, is that you?"

"Good morning, Mrs. Facetti, how are you today?"

"Good morning, young man. I'm fine, thank you. And thank you for the rent."

Thanks to Senior, my rent was always paid a week early. I pushed Ray back in front of his bowl of milk, making sure he had his eyes off my piece of cake

"Yes, ma'am, you're welcome."

"What are you up to today?"

"Off to school, I guess."

Mrs. Facetti entered the kitchen from the back room pantry, wearing a black dress, holding the tomatoes that she had canned from the past summer in the well of her apron. Reaching up, I bent to let her kiss me on my forehead. Making her way to the stove, she stopped and turned. "It's Thursday, Stevie, I'm making sauce today. Stop by Mr. Lombardi's and pick up two loaves of bread for me, please. Take fifty cents from my dish." She continued to the stove, not missing a beat. Then over her shoulder, "You're such a sweet boy, you should be with your parents, Stevie. It's not safe for you to be on your own at fifteen years old. You saw what happened to your cousin Bobby."

"Yes, ma'am. Thank you. I'll be fine, really. I speak to my folks and see my family from time to time. I have a lot of friends." She stopped and turned again, pulling me close, taking me by both hands. Looking me in the eye she said, "Listen to me, these people, they are not friends, Stevie. They will lead you into trouble if they haven't already. I know Senior is a good and respectful man, and Tony and you are close. But let me ask one of my sons to fix you up at the market packing bags after school, OK?"

I bent down, kissing her hands still cupped in mine. They smelled of Dial soap and basil. "Sure, Mrs. Facetti, that would be great."

The Lombardi's had the best bakery on the Lower East Side for three generations, over on Bleecker Street. They also paid protection to Senior. Every Thursday I would stop by for two loaves of fresh baked Italian bread, a pat on the shoulder, and an envelope with fifty dollars, a white cardboard box tied with string, full of biscotti, and a ten-dollar tip for my trouble.

"You tell Senior how we always treat you with respect, Stevie."

"Yes, sir, Mr. Lombardi, I will. Thank you for the cookies."

On my return I was greeted by the smells of fresh-squeezed tomatoes, garlic, and three different meats cooking together in harmony in a big cast iron pot on Mrs. Facetti's stove. Lifting the lid, the window behind the stove became foggy as the steam rose from the pot. Ripping off a hunk of warm bread, I dipped it into the simmering red. Before me, the bread soaked up the thick, sweet sauce. Stuffing the entire piece of bread in my mouth with a meatball, dropping the ten dollars Mr. Lombardi gave me and her fifty cents back in her dish, I headed for the door . . .

"You're going to choke, Stevie. Slow down, and take a plate next time. Sit and eat." With a smile in her voice she continued, "And please, sweetie, stop leaving me money."

"Mrs. Facetti?"

"Yes, Stevie?"

"Love you."

"Love you too, silly boy." Laughing, "Be careful."

"Yes, ma'am."

JANUARY 2, 1970

It was freezing outside. I came back from Lombardi's that day, having said good-bye to Mrs. Facetti less than two hours before, promising her I'd be right back. As I turned onto Eldridge Street, I saw the cops and ambulances in front of my building. I pushed forward, past the whispers and stares of my neighbors. I knew instinctively it wasn't good.

Mrs. Facetti's door sat wide open. In her kitchen, a pool of blood was soaking into the floor, mixing with the tomato sauce, the empty pot and pieces of meat scattered across the floor. One of our neighbors was crying, holding Big Ray. His neck broken. Still warm and limp, his warm, once soft multi-colored fur was now matted, covered in his owner's sauce and blood. Mrs. Facetti's body lay on the floor covered with a white sheet, now partially red, matching the growing stain spreading on the floor beneath her. One hand and part of her black dress peeking out from underneath the sheet's edges.

A junkie had gotten into the building, hoping to lift anything he could find and then sell or trade it to buy dope. He had found Mrs. Facetti's door unlocked, with just the safety chain keeping it closed. He pushed the door in, pulling the screw out of the soft wood of the front door. He then proceeded to beat the woman to death with his fists and feet. Then he killed Ray, evidently for attacking him and clawing his face as he beat his master and friend to a pulp.

People blocks away remember seeing a guy running down the street from our direction, holding his right cheek as blood poured from between his fingers, leaving a trail on the pavement. Ray was a big boy and must have really dug in with both his mouth and claws.

This scumbag, who unknowingly became the walking dead, pried the wedding ring off the dead old woman's finger. He then took a bracelet she had from childhood off the right wrist of her lifeless, beaten body. Worthless pieces of jewelry to anyone but her. All this, not realizing she had the month's rent for the entire building, totaling fourteen hundred dollars, held to the back of her apron with a safety-pin in a small brown envelope. For kicks on his way out, he had taken the time to pour the boiling tomato sauce all over her and Ray before he ran. All he had to do was ask her if she had any money and she would have handed over the collected month's rent without a fuss and then offered him a plate of food.

By the time Tony arrived, he was in a state that I had never seen, barely keeping it together. Jerry tried his best to talk him down, then leaned in and told me quietly to go to Senior's and wait with him until they returned from wherever they were going. They pulled away in Jerry's Buick and disappeared down Eldridge, turning left onto Delancey. Looking for a junkie with cuts on his face, tomato sauce on his clothing, fencing stolen jewelry.

Tony had known Mrs. Facetti since he was a baby. After Tony's mom died, getting hit by a car on Second Avenue that ran a red-light, Mrs. Facetti had become his mother. Within hours, he called Senior from a payphone and told him they had found the guy. They had found his dealer, who after a bit of persuasion and a busted jaw, gave Fat Jerry the address of where the shitbag lived over on Hester Street. Two hours later Fat Jerry and Tony delivered the partially intact piece of crap to Senior's place on Mulberry Street. When they lifted him out of the trunk, he was spitting blood and crying, begging to be let go. He already had a busted nose, one eye beat shut, and was bleeding big time from what was left of his right ear, which seemed to be hanging on by a small piece of skin. This is where Big Ray had dug in deep with claws and teeth. It looked like two of the guy's fingers were broken from getting caught when he got thrown into the trunk of the Buick and Jerry closed the lid, not giving a shit. I watched Tony and Jerry beat him to his knees. Then Senior poured boiling water on his arms and hands. I was made to stand there. Transfixed in horror, I was unable to move anyhow. The guy's skin turned red, buckled, peeled, and then seemed to crack like hot asphalt. Killing him would save him the pain of living like this. Ending his time on planet Earth was too easy.

His screams of pain were worthless currency in payment for what he had done to a member of our family. In Senior's world, he had crossed a line. *The Line.* Killing an old woman who did nothing and who instead cared about the people in her building and community for fifty-five years, who trusted everyone and who we loved as family, needlessly murdered. When the guy finally passed out from the pain, they wrapped him in a beach blanket, threw him back in the trunk for a second and last time and dumped him at the bottom of Allen Street. Mrs. Facetti's two sons silently came by that same night and cleaned out our matriarch's flat, leaving nothing behind but the stains of her blood on the linoleum, the faint smell of tomato sauce, and Big Ray's bowl of milk. Now soured and alone.

One week later, that same junkie mugged an old man on Stanton Street. Bandages still covering his blistered fuckin' arms and hands. One patch over his right eye and another over what was left of his ear when he beat our local ragman, Mr. Jacoby, half to death for six fuckin' dollars and his Timex watch. Last time we saw that broken sack of shit junkie, he was being put in the trunk of Jerry's Buick for the third and final time, on his way to Prince Street for flying lessons from what I heard but could never confirm. You know how things get exaggerated sometimes?

JACK ABRAMOWITZ
SPRING, 1970

Early morning, especially pre-dawn, has always been a certain, and most days, an exclusive time of day for me. Before the world rises and scatters the peace that night left behind as a gift. That almost light kind of darkness before daylight burns the last shadows away. New York City was the land of magic back in 1970. At five-forty-five in the morning downtown on the Lower East Side, for me, it was pure wizardry.

Lighting my first of many joints to follow, sipping my morning tea purchased for a nickel at the bakery on the south side of Canal Street in Chinatown, I winded my way down to Fulton Street Fish Market. High and warmed by the tea, I dumped the roach from the joint into the empty teacup and deposited them both into a metal wire garbage can sitting on the corner. Finally, crossing Water Street to my final destination. The sounds and smells were welcoming. It was one of my favorite places to go when I can't sleep from constant nightmares. The floors of the market were slick and wet due to fish scales, guts, and the ice melting around all the fish in small bins, waiting to either be sold whole or butchered right there. Finding a dry spot on the dock, sitting at the edge, able to dangle my feet six feet above the water, I lit a cigarette and drew a deep drag. I exhaled and contemplated the smoke drifting away over my head. Watching the boats come in with the catch of the day and pull away unloaded and empty, they sit higher on the water as they slip past, leaving me behind. I'm content watching the sunrise over the East River. Carrying the day's heat and expectations with it.

Jack Abramowitz saw me first, hanging around the market, looking to lift some fish. A rat can always smell another rat. As he approached me, he had the look of a dog that had been kicked just enough to make him bite if you moved too fast or the wrong way. He smelled of fish, his apron stained with scales and guts. We introduced ourselves, came to terms, shook hands, and cut a deal in ten minutes.

Monday mornings before 8:00, he would leave a large burlap sack in an open cardboard box stuffed with the catch of the day behind the trash bin on the corner of Water and Wall Streets. I would walk by and pick up the box of fish, then sell them in Chinatown, seven blocks north, pocketing the cash for myself. I supplied him with one of Senior's winning numbers, which I left written in pencil on a piece of brown paper under a brick, behind the same trash bin. He never asked what I was doing with the fish, and I never asked how he got them.

Senior knew about my fishing trips to the waterfront, as well as the numbers I was supplying Jack each week, long before I knew that he knew. Senior knew everything. One day at the club, he was sitting at the end of the bar watching baseball, drinking a beer, and smoking a cigar. As always, looking like a million dollars. Without turning away from the game, he said, "Ask your new friend Jack to stop by the club tonight. I'll have Jerry pick him up."

I had learned not to react to anything Senior said. Just listen and obey. He knew all about our side gigs and never said a thing. If we kept it clean and to ourselves and showed respect. He had discovered who Jack was after finding out about our little deal from his connection in Chinatown who saw me selling a box of fish to one of the fishmongers on Mott Street. Senior had decided Jack might be the type of guy he was looking for regarding, as Senior put it, "Something I need to take care of personally."

That evening Jerry and I picked Jack up at his dump over on Clinton Street and drove him to Senior's club on Mulberry. Seeing me in the car sitting up front next to Big Jerry, he knew it was safe and got in. Still, understandably nervous as to why someone like Senior would want to see a guy like him.

When we got to the club, Senior sat waiting at the big table in the middle of the room. A lit cigarette comfortably resting in the corner of his mouth. The light fixture above the table sucked in the exhaled smoke from his lungs like a magnet. Ashtray, pack of Parliaments, and a square silver lighter, neatly laid out in front of him, from left to right.

Locking all of us in for the duration, Fat Jerry slid the latch home as we took our places. Church-like, me and Tony walked to "our spot" and settled in. A small half round padded booth with an even smaller, clean table placed in front. Jerry took his usual post, sitting on a bar stool watching the traffic, pedestrian and otherwise, out a small, tinted window.

"Jack, sit down. You know who I am?"

"Yes, I do. Everyone knows who you are, Senior."

"Can I get you something to drink? Beer, stronger?" Senior had heard Jack might have a drinking problem.

"No, thank you, Senior, I'm good."

"I'm going to ask you a very personal question. Is that all right, Jack?"

A small crack in his voice, "Of course, Senior."

Senior moved closer, whispering in Jack's ear, continuing, menacingly, "Did you ever think about settling down?"

"YOU MEAN GET MARRIED!!??" Jack realized his animated response had changed the energy in the room. He took a deep breath and probably wished at that moment he had said yes to that drink Senior had offered. He replied, much calmer, "No, it never crossed my mind." Jack started sweating. His posture, rigor mortis. Appropriate, considering, in his mind's eye, his life, as he knew it, might be over wielding the inertia of a slow-moving freight train (if you get where I'm going here). The floor was still Senior's. I sat there in awe, watching a street-level species of spider catch a not so smart fly for its next meal.

"You know, Jack, there is opportunity in everything; a steady income, a friendly place to lay your head at night, maybe even a bit of protection, if you understand where I'm goin' here. Our dear friend Larry lost his father. He needs a dad, and his mom needs a husband. You know how that goes. A boy needs a man's influence, a hand on his shoulder, if you will. To guide him toward his own manhood. Of course, help paying the bills, things like that. His mom, Denise, is a good Polish woman of faith. She can keep the right man happy."

Senior then moved his chair a bit closer, turned and faced Jack dead on eye to eye, then continued without missing a beat, "They need a solid kinda guy like you around the house." It was time for the spider to start feeding off the fly it had ensnared. "I'm sure Stevie told you all about the last time he gave you the winning numbers."

Senior legitimately paused, this time to light a Newport. His ritual now complete, he looked at Jack and said, "So, Jack, I ask you . . . are you *that* kinda guy?"

Jack swiveled around and glared at me, thinking I set him up. He knew it was blackmail. If he didn't comply and bend to whatever Senior asked, he would have to pay back months' worth of winnings that he had cheated to get because of me, plus the vig.[*]

Senior sauntered toward me in an alpha strut and smiled, patted me on the cheek, and whispered, "Next time tell me before you make deals with my numbers and go to Chinatown to sell fish."

The message was a compost of a father's love and don't ever embarrass me on the street or fuck with me like this again.

---

[*] Short for vigorish. An absurd fee applied to money owed, not from a bank.

Everything he said to me in the years we spent as family were all lessons, but this was a warning.

Jack sat staring at the door, wishing it open, freeing him from his inevitable conclusion. You never say no to Senior. You could, but why do that to yourself?

Larry's dad (I don't remember his first name) died in 1967 of a heart attack during a bank robbery at Crosslands Savings up on 14th and Sixth Avenue while he was making a deposit for his boss. That left Larry and his mom Denise without any savings and now no income.

Senior and Larry's dad had grown up together on the same block as kids and stayed friends through the years. Knowingly never asking questions of the other's life and greeting each other warmly, asking about each other's family. Always a reciprocated hug good-bye.

Every Christmas, Fat Jerry would deliver two crisp one-hundred-dollar bills slipped under the door in an unmarked envelope.

Senior wasn't a complicated man; you always knew where you stood with him. He could be generous. In retrospect, most of him was dark and violent.

Out of true affection, Senior felt responsible for taking care of Larry and his mom until he could figure something more suitable, more sustainable. It had been years of paying the bills and watching over her and Larry. So . . .

Three weeks after Jack's visit to the club, on a Sunday afternoon, Jack Abramowitz and Larry's mom, Mrs. Denise Lipschitz, got married in a temple over on Clinton Street at Congregation Chasem Sopher, a congregation formed back in 1892 by Polish immigrants.

Everyone was there, all bathed and washed. All except our treasured surrogate, Mrs. Facetti. For me, the way she and Big Ray were slaughtered left an insufferable hole in my heart and my head every time I walked past her front door, never again to pass through it into her world, a world where I felt safe. I had let my guard down; I should have been there instead of taking so long. Naively, I believed she was untouchable, a saint, that monsters were scared of her power. I was so very wrong...

Senior had Dominic close his place that Sunday afternoon. Pizza, Italian heroes, salad, Pepsi, and red wine. Fresh cannoli and ricotta cheesecake with small dark cups of espresso. Frank Sinatra on the jukebox. Everyone eating and laughing, dancing, and having a blast. There were people there I had never seen before. Friends of Seniors, each handing an envelope to one of the newlyweds, placing it in a white lace sack with a soft kiss on the check and a handshake. I watched Jack most of the time. He tried his best, talking, dancing with the bride. Doing his best to be the new husband. I thought I saw him pocket one of the envelopes. You never steal from your own. This guy would need some watching.

At this point, dear reader, I will admit that this was a colossal mistake on Senior's part, the way I saw it. Jack was not the type of guy Senior wanted in any way. Senior had him on the hook for a small sum of 10K, which is what Senior had assessed based on the deal I had made with Jack. This 10K also accumulated interest. But some guys are just stupid, so stupid in fact that they are able to hide it, fearing someone will find out. Knowing that they are just that stupid. But in the end, you know what they say, "Stupid is as stupid does." What the fuck had Senior been thinking? I kept it to myself. Telling not a soul. Especially Junior. I knew Jack would eventually crash and burn. But some things were not open for discussion under penalty of extreme discomfort. So, I stepped outside and fired up a joint, filed my insights away, went back inside and partied my ass off ...

Jack moved into Larry's third-floor flat on Hester Street. It seemed like a blessing for a while. One big happy family for almost a year. I was beginning to think I was wrong. Then two things happened. Jack started drinking more than usual, and the shit hit the fan.

"Mom, what happened to your arm? It's all bruised."

"Nothing, Larry, I walked into the door carrying the laundry upstairs."

That afternoon as Jack got home from work at the fish market, Larry stopped him outside their building as we sat on the stoop across the street and watched. He had cleared it with Tony already. "You ever touch my mother again, I'll fuckin' kill you, motherfucker. You have no right to harm her. She is a good woman; she suffered enough, you piece of shit."

Bean was right up in Jack's face. Jack turned red, grabbed Larry, shook him like a rag doll, and gave him a black eye. Tony said sit, so we did. Jack was screaming now, emboldened, *She is my property now, same as you. I will do what I want when I want, so fuck off! God knows I can't stand having you around me anyway, you're a fuckin' little worm!* He stopped and turned toward us, *Fuck your friends, as well, sitting across the street. Senior gave me his blessing. The deal is done,* turning to us and giving us a robust middle finger.

Tony placed his hand on my shoulder. "Let it play out, Stevie." He knew if I didn't get up, neither would anyone else. But if I did make a move, there would be no stopping my onslaught. *Swing Stevie, swing away, get up, go, baby, go* . . . So, I sat there shaking like a racehorse at the starting gate ready to spring, Tony's hand on my shoulder.

That is how it began. Jack would walk into Larry's room in the middle of the night, punching him awake, placing his hand over his mouth and telling him what he had just done to his mom in bed, as tears of frustration and pain rolled down Larry's face. This went on for weeks. Then the cracks started showing. Larry was not stupid and knew a lot of people. Back in those days, there was always someone to do what needed to be done to someone else for the right price.

One morning as Jack walked to work, he was pulled into an alley on Essex Street by three guys wearing ski masks. In the space of five minutes, they tuned him up to the point of forty-five stitches on his leg, a busted nose, two broken fingers, a black eye, and two fractured ribs. Larry's nightly beatings stopped as Jack healed. But hate and revenge were now in full play. Jack stopped torturing Larry physically, but the mournful sounds from his mom's bedroom hurt much deeper than the blows that landed on his stomach and legs. His mom got the full brunt of his stepfather's anger. This drove Larry mad. He would knock on my door late into the night, escaping from the sounds of whimpering, beatings, and forced sex inflicted on his mom. We would sit there in my flat, stone cold quiet. He would fall asleep and be off in the morning before I woke. All he or I had to do was tell Senior and it would have all stopped. But we never did. He made me promise not to. He would take care of it, for good this time.

One night as Jack lay on the sofa drunk and passed out, Larry got really drunk and poured lighter fluid on his private parts and lit him on fire. Jack's pants and the sofa caught fire and started to really cook before he woke up smelling the burning denim of his jeans and the heat on his three-piece set. It was enough to push Jack over the edge.

AN ODD AND VIOLENT ABSTRACT DESIGN

SEPTEMBER, 1970

Jerry's chestnut brown, shiny, new Buick sedan glided up to the curb in front of my stoop. Windows down, the back door already opening. Tony yelled out, "Come on, get in. We're going for a ride, kid." Some things you never said no to. I got in. We floated east down Houston Street and got onto the FDR Drive heading north. Five minutes later we were smoking a joint and listening to some indescribable song on WCBS-FM with all the windows down doing sixty-five miles an hour with no seatbelts.

Tony and Big Jerry were going on a collection run uptown. Collections were made without question. It was regarded as a sign of great trust to handle that amount of cash. We exited at 34th Street. Headed west to Broadway, up to 39th Street. The Garment District. I waited in the car with Junior as Jerry made the rounds in the different buildings. He tipped every janitor, elevator, and maintenance guy he found. Making sure they all knew that this was the better of two options. Keeping one's eyes shut for twenty dollars was better than getting one's head split open for free.

Two hours later we drove back downtown with the trunk of Jerry's Buick full of mink coats and a bag of cash. The mink coats were compliments of Mr. Ira Cohen and his famous Mink Palace. The envelopes containing the month's take of eighty-six thousand dollars representing a combination of protection money and trash removal. We headed back downtown. Jerry exited the FDR and made the right onto Grand Street.

We made it to the corner of Eldridge Street just in time to see the all too familiar and repeated performance of ambulance attendants covering another body.

Our friend Larry the Bean's body was in a blanket this time and being loaded into the back of the ambulance. He was shot in the back of the head as he walked home from the grocery store. His blood, milk, and pieces of his brain and hair, mixing in an odd and violent abstract design against the curb. The bullet had ripped into the center of his head, splitting his glasses in two as it exited out through the bridge of his nose. By the time we got there, Larry's blood, brains, and milk had started drying where his body had fallen. Junior covered the jigsaw puzzle remains with the sports pages of the morning's *Daily News* that he found in the garbage. The Yankees had won the night before. Their victory now colored dark red. A photo of the winning home run by Bobby Mercer in the eighth inning with two men on becoming unrecognizable as the newspaper soaked up the history of what just happened. We knew right away who had pulled the trigger. Everyone on the street that morning saw Jack Abramowitz fire the shot into the back of his head and run.

A week after the shooting, Junior and I sat on our stoop waiting for the other shoe to drop. One afternoon the Buick slowly rolled around the corner. Jerry gently pulled up to the curb without saying hello. Jack was shooting dice against the building across the street with his guys, drinking from a brown paper bag, laughing, and smoking a joint as if nothing had happened.

Jerry hit the button, rolling down the back-left window. Senior sat there, dressed to the nines. Sunglasses, thin leather gloves, a gun resting on his lap. We all knew there was a plastic tarp, bricks, and rope in the trunk. Senior's face was a death mask. He felt responsible for the way things had turned out. He had made an intractable mistake and was set on making things right, his way. We all held our breath. Fear had just turned down the volume on everything else except Senior's voice. "Jack, get in the car. We need to talk."

Jack froze, his eyes moving wildly from left to right, visibly vibrating with fear, "Senior, please, the kid had me beaten up, then the little bastard set me on fire. He could have burned down the building. I'm sorry, Senior."

Ignoring Jack completely, Senior said loud enough for everyone to hear, "Jerry, please place our dear friend Jack in the front seat next to you, thank you." Seamlessly, Fat Jerry dropped the car into park. Walking over to Jack, he politely opened the door for him to get in. I remember how small Jack looked as they drove west to the Holland Tunnel. We never saw Jack again.

Larry did not deserve to die. He never hurt anyone. If Senior hadn't taken care of things, we would have. Senior knew Tony and me and what we were capable of and would have done with Jack. He beat us to it, saving the neighborhood from unwanted attention and more blood spilled needlessly onto his streets.

Later that evening when Jerry and Senior returned, we pretended nothing happened. Senior looked unhappy; Jerry looked relieved. Larry's mom was placed in a two-bedroom apartment in Little Italy on the corner of Mott and Hester and taken care of for the rest of her days. Her rent paid. The day we helped her move into her new apartment, we all sat there and cried – Junior, Fat Jerry, and me.

How cool and awful it would have been to see Jack Abramowitz, his limp and broken body, a bullet in the back of his head, his body wrapped in the plastic tarp tied with cord and bricks and dumped in the water... sinking into the swamps of New Jersey, I presume. Who really knows? You know the urban myths. For all we know, Jack Abramowitz could be alive and well, living in Ohio under a different name.

BOOK TWO
DRAMATIS PERSONAE

"Someone I loved once gave me a box full of darkness. It took me years to understand that this, too, was a gift."

Mary Oliver

WELLCOME TO BOOK TWO

If we've gotten this far together, that's a good thing. That means you made it to the end of Book One. Bravo. It was a motherfucker to write it all down and reveal it all, to give something like that the light of day after so many decades. Hopefully the same adjective applied as you read it. I thought perhaps that you'd like to read something less violent and more revealing in Book Two. There were, to my good fortune, significantly dear and important men in my life as a child and into early adulthood. Most real family. Some called family. You've already met Tony, Senior, and Fat Jerry in Book One.

As you will read, there was another side to my childhood. Before I decided to run away. A balance, filled with unconditional love, music, joy, and a huge sense of safety, when I was able to get to it.

As things changed and went downhill through my tween years to my early teens, my life would become filled with love and lies to those closest to me. Hoping I could build a narrative on something more normal. Hiding from the world my true self and the pain *that never dissipated. Both emotional and physical. The pages of Book Two are bits and pieces. Stories of who I am now based on the lessons, trials, and love I was shown as a child. Then through the experiences I was blessed to have been a part of, I somehow made it work . . .*

The Author

MOTHER

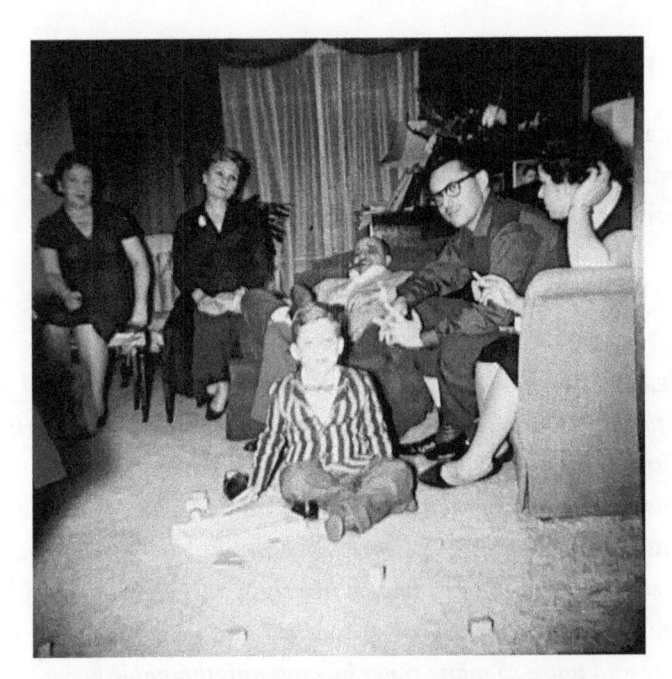

Queens, New York, 1959. (My father's parents' apartment. Grandpa Abe taking the photo.) Every Sunday for thirty years, we gathered there. Sunday dinner was a big deal and a safe, happy place.

MONSTER

One who deviates from normal or acceptable behavior or character, an immoral monster, a threatening force, something monstrous, especially a person of unnatural or extreme ugliness to form a wickedness or cruelty.

RAPE

That which is snatched away to perform an action causing results harmful or unpleasant to a person or thing. Unlawful sexual activity, and usually sexual intercourse, carried out forcibly or under threat of injury against a person's will or with a person who is beneath a certain age or incapable of valid consent because of mental illness.

MOTHER

Maternal tenderness or affection, short for mother fucker, sometimes vulgar, mother fucker.
    Merriam-Webster, 2022 (source of definitions).

The biggest issue for my first editor and myself was to find a final destination for the following pages. After reading my manuscript, they gently asked me if I could write more explicitly about my repeated rape and abuse... Okay. The memories are unhealable. There is still admixture and synthesis in lighting, the smell of "Mr. Bubble" bubble bath, and certain color towels. The foul images awash in my head can never be recycled into anything reusable. I was touched and penetrated and made to penetrate and touch so many times in ways unfathomable between mother and son.

    The subjugation of my childhood has become segregated from who I was as a human being, in this world, and as a man. If these retrospections reassert themselves by some fault of my own, I am able to turn their power off, like an electronic device, and they go silent.

The Author

CONTEMPLATING DEATH, KODACHROME, AND PHONE BOOKS

1961

My parents owned a children's clothing store on Austin Street in Forest Hills, Queens, called The Little Shop. Some nightmares, when I used to entertain them, took place on Austin Street. My father and grandfather Moe opened it together, a partnership from 1962 through 1965. To help bail out my father once again from everything he failed at. My father also drove a cab at night.

Most times it was just me and the monster, even when things seemed normal, like doing homework, watching the news, eating Swanson TV dinners, or obsessing over Saturday morning cartoons. (My favorite thing ever as a kid. Out in public, with family or friends, we were one big bunch of happy motherfuckers.)

"Smile, Stevie! What's wrong?"

CAKE AND NICOTINE
1962

"*Mom . . . MOM!?*" Stubbing her cigarette in her dessert plate, springing from my grandmother's dining room table, she hurled herself across the room. Grabbing me by my arm, spitting out her words, she whispered roughly in my ear, "Shut the fuck up, Stevie, or I swear I'll slap your shitty little ass quiet . . . go turn on the fucking TV in the fucking living room, and no *Three Stooges,* they are too violent . . . Do you hear me?" Shaking me back and forth by the arm for effect, "I will deal with you when we get home." Broken, I shuffled over to the TV rubbing my arm, wiping her spit out of my ear, refusing to cry, smelling of cake and nicotine. Sitting on the floor, hands between my legs, playing with myself in my grandmother's living room, watching animals devour each other on *Mutual Kingdom* on her new color TV because the *Three Stooges* in black and white was too violent.

The TV remote control made a kind of *cath-wanging,* springy sound that vibrated in my hand every time I pushed one of the brown oval buttons . . . over and over, again and again. Then my grandmother Mina's calm Russian lilted voice, "Stevie, darling, please don't sit that close to the TV. The color is bad for your eyes, and stop pushing the buttons on the remote, you'll break it!"

Rocking back and forth, arms and legs crossed in frustration, joyfully as possible.

"Yes, Grandma." Things in my life are one big cluster fuck. I am seven years old.

1962

We had just moved into a new apartment building, "The Arlington." Our doorman, Scotty, purposefully standing, ready to spring into action. Guarding our building, opening the door, and directing the deliveries to the basement. In his dark navy doorman uniform, complete with gold braided epaulets on his shoulders to match the gold braid banding around his army-style dress hat. Captain Scotty, every little kid's buddy, who always had shiny eyes and smelled of beer.

We lived in a two-bedroom apartment on the fourth floor. My room had a window that faced a U-shaped courtyard below. It was filled with flowerpots and paths with benches off to the side, all placed in and around the newly planted shade trees.

The window was open. No one had child guards back then, just thin screens to keep the bugs out. I slid the screen up, placing my hands on the sill of the window. I peered down feeling the wonderful feeling of letting go, saying, "*Sayonara*" to all the pain and lies. It would only take the slip of my hands to tumble out and down. Instead, I took every toy, lamp, chair, and loose object that was not nailed down and gave them the gift of flight. The benches and bushes became covered with the juvenile debris of my young, sick life. A sizable crowd of children and adults gathered, staring up, shouting and laughing at me at the top of their lungs, looking like little battery-operated dolls. Later that day, I vividly remember a neighbor bringing a small white box full of unbroken wreckage to our apartment door and my mother thanking her. Surprised at not hearing what I had done only twenty feet away behind the closed door of my room, she beat the shit out of me with one of the unbroken toys. The next day, I went to school and threw a chalkboard eraser at the teacher's back. Her dress, covered in white chalk, made all the other kids laugh. My mother came to school and picked me up at the principal's office. She smacked me all the way home in the car. When we got there, she beat me with a small local Yellow Pages phone book only to lock me in the closet for an hour. I remember being led out of the closet after sitting in utter darkness as the lock clicked back and the door swung open.

It was one of those beautiful overly bright summer afternoons. Kodachrome.

1963

Photo booth, Summer, 1962.

Now, at nine years old, physical abuse, verbal abuse, or both. Exposing me to my mother's will and timing with no place for me to hide. There was never any real rest. Only when my father was home was there any reprieve. But my father was never home. He left before

I got up for school in the morning, and since he worked two jobs, he always came home after I was already in bed at night. I dreamed of being chased by witches and monsters. Running naked through the streets of my neighborhood. Opening my mouth to scream, with no voice for anyone to hear my cry for help. At times, the weight of fear was more than my young brain could hold. During her abuse, I learned to leave my body to a land of detachment. Still, I loved my mother dearly; and in equal parts at the same time, I entertained thoughts of different ways to kill her.

Port Washington, New York. Louie's seafood restaurant, Summer, 1963.

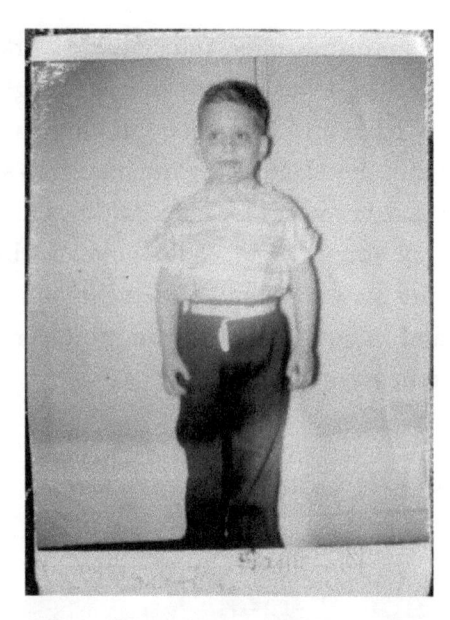

Not sure when or where this was taken. I must be about four years old.

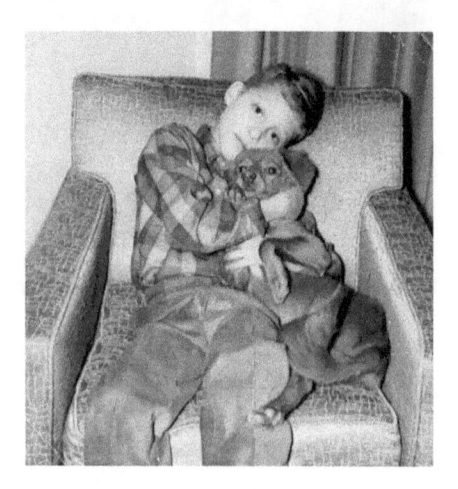

Jamaica, Queens, 1966. Me and Fluffy (my first dog) on our favorite chair. My dad took this photo. I actually remember it vividly. It was on a Sunday in the fall.

CAKE AND NICOTINE • 67

1965 in front of the Arlington. Me, my dad holding Fluffy, my sister in the background. My mom took the photo.

CLOWNS IN THE CLOSET
1964

I was ten years old. My grandfather took me to the circus every spring when it came to the old Madison Square Garden on Eighth Avenue between 49th and 50th Streets. He always bought me one of those small circus flashlights. The flashlight had a red flip-top that turned on its light when you popped back the top; it had bright red circus clowns beautifully painted on its sides. It came with a long red plastic cord, so you could twirl it over your head when the arena lights went out. At home, I would hide the flashlight and my toy soldiers in a small cloth bag in the back of the hallway closet. It was there for me when my mother locked me in after her abuse and beatings. Always stuffing a towel under the door to black out the light completely.

Dad also placed his *National Geographic* in the closet in a pile on the floor, meant to have been thrown out when he was done reading them. They would sit there for months before disappearing, only to be replaced by newer ones. Locked in the dark, the mothballs making my eyes water, sore and angry from what I had just endured, I would use my circus flashlight to pass the time looking at the pictures in these wonderful magazines. Playing with my toy soldiers, turning the pages, wondering where these places were and how different it must be for the kids who lived there. Stewing over the idea of putting rat poison in my mother's morning coffee and watching her die as I stood there brought a sick grin to my lips. Me and my clowns in the closet. Sitting together in the dark, smiling at the thought of murdering my own mother. There were no cute tales or happy conclusions when it comes to my mother. She plowed through life and everything and everyone in her way . . . including me. She was a fucking animal. So, now you know.

ALICE BEING ALICE - PART 1

Alice was born in the thriving Jewish community of North Lawndale, Chicago, in 1935. Moving to New York sometime before she was ten years old. Grandpa Moe Rahmey moved his tribe into a large single-family home in a middle-class Jewish enclave of Forest Hills, Queens. My grandma Ruth had a history of having an *"addictive personality."* By the time she married my grandfather at the age of twenty-years old, there was a list of emergency room visits for overdosing on pills and liquor. At one point, there was talk of a short-term, in-patient care facility for troubled young women. Marrying my grandfather saved her and her family from that fate.

My grandfather was a haberdasher by trade, working as a salesman for Marshall Fields in Chicago, selling gloves and hats for both men and women. After six years of trying to make it work and not seeing a future for his family, my grandfather felt there was opportunity and money to be made in New York. So, he schlepped everyone east. Moved to Queens and opened a haberdashery store in Manhattan on 34th Street, directly across from the Empire State Building.

My mother had a framed, parchment yellow four-by-eight newspaper story clipped from some tabloid of the day. It was on every nightstand she ever slept next to, I remember that vividly. When she passed away I looked everywhere for it, to no avail. I'm sure its packed away somewhere, unless she took it with her to the eternal nightstand in the sky.

The article involved an eleven-year-old little girl who, while hiding behind the inventory in her father's haberdashery shop one day, watched in horror as two well-dressed men robbed him. In this posed photographic re-enactment of the reported crime, it showed a 1940's Shirley Temple style little girl in an expensive dress, with perfect hair tied in a bow, her face displaying mock concern and fear as she timidly peered around the boxes of hats and gloves witnessing the whole event. Holding her hand over her "Oh my!" oval-shaped mouth ... brave little Alice.

Alice's mother, my grandmother. Unfortunately, Ruth took her addiction with her when she packed and left for New York. My grandfather had hoped the move would help cure her addictions. Instead, it thrived as they settled into their new life in Queens, and she did not give a shit whether people knew or not. Grandma Ruth suffered from deep depression, with huge mood swings. Grandpa Moe was her enabler, giving her condition permission to thrive. Buying her flowers and jewelry, telling her everything was okay and how much he loved her, which he did. He loved her so much that he filled all her prescriptions for antidepressants and sleeping pills. Having all the alcohol she consumed delivered in controlled amounts to the apartment. Giving her only what pills she needed to get through the day, taking the rest with him to work. Sedating her just enough, knowing the live-in housekeeper or nanny would give her the custodial care she needed until he returned home at the end of the day. As the rest of us through the years gradually entered the picture, as a family we mostly put up with her screaming, four-letter insults, and her harmful behavior only when it was absolutely necessary, i.e., funerals, weddings, and bar mitzvahs. Other times, she was politely told to shut up and to please sit the fuck down by my mother and my aunt, her sister... which worked out well, when we were out and about as a family, being she always wanted to leave fifteen-minutes after she got there anyway. As her depression and addiction took hold of her, my mother and Aunt Ellen skillfully pretended there was nothing to talk about, going on with what they had been doing. They did this while simultaneously plying her with drinks and platitudes to shut her up, which never made much sense to me both as a child and now as an adult. At my bar mitzvah, she got so fucked up that they carried her out... *"It's fine, we're all leaving soon anyway... You should see her if she doesn't drink!"*

Witnessing my grandmother's drunken, chemically-induced stupors and rage, her abusive and addictive behavior was a deeply dysfunctional and damaging blow in the head for my mother growing up. Both inside and out. My aunt would tell me of the enduring screaming insults and beatings with a hairbrush when Moe was at work that Ruth seemed to aim directly at young Alice. I know grandmother's behavior and abuse on my mother was supremely evident in the way my mother beat and abused me. I have since come to believe it was jealousy over my grandfather's attention toward her, just as my mother's jealousy over the fuss everyone made over my being born drove her crazy, after she did all the work directing her sick behavior toward me. I have to say Alice, being the animal she was, conveyed her anger and her pain to me and on me on a whole other fuckin' level.

ALICE BEING ALICE - PART II

Wielding her drama and bravado all the time, as a child I watched my mother hold court. Every time we were out and everywhere we went, she was front and center.

Alice's speeches at the Borodkin's Sunday dinner table held every weekend ceremoniously at my dad's folks' place. Once sufficiently lubed with liquor, like her mother, her droning sloppy soliloquies were legendary. Pontificating on and on in between puffs on her Newport, the filter covered in shiny red lipstick. Robotically sipping Harvey's Bristol Cream on the rocks from a large tumbler displaying a matching red mark on its rim.

She would go on and on about how she loved her life with little Stevie and her man, my amazing and deeply damaged father. *"Oh, my Stevie is such a darling little boy, and my Howie! He is such a good father and husband."* My ghost of a father sitting there listening, smiling, chain smoking, drinking scotch, and developing stomach ulcers and eventually cancer. He was as much in the dark as I was sitting in the closet.

Alice had the foulest mouth, highest hair, and the brightest lipstick. For my mother, life was a cocktail mix of looking good, cooking, drinking, and holding down the fort at home while my dad worked nights driving a cab. She slept with most of my dad's friends while he went out and busted his ass putting food on our plates.

I remember as a kid sitting at the top of the stairs watching my dad and his friends play cards on Wednesday nights, and my mom serving food, watching the guys stare at her tits, each thinking about how nice it's gonna be to get their hands on them again.

My dad, oblivious to what was going on, drinking and sucking on a Marlboro, happy as shit. (Which in the end was completely the opposite and another story). There were no cute tales or happy conclusions when it came to my mother. She plowed through life and everything and everyone in her way... including me.

FATHER

My dad was a constant pillar whose façade and structure cracked and crumbled over and over again, rebuilding itself in its own image before finally turning into dust forever. My dad's musical heart and his intellect. His pitiful sadness and displays of weakness. His music and his Marlboros. I watched my mother slowly poison him with her mere presence, disgusting behavior, and final reasons for their divorce.

So, instead of running from my mother like I had, he stayed and smoked himself to death . . . fuckin' cancer. Through each of our trials and our mistakes over the decades, my father and I never turned our backs on each other in anger. Yes, we had our moments, as you can imagine. But we always came together, one to the other, the other always accepting.

My father, who never said good-bye, instead always said, "See you later, kiddo, love you, so proud of you." Lately, when I stare into the mirror, I see a lot of my father looking back at me.

So be it. Miss you, Dad.

My father and I are in the empty lot across from Grandma Mina and Grandpa Abe's apartment. I'm holding my baby sister's tippy cup. My Grandpa Abe took the picture.

EIGHTY-EIGHT KEYS AND THE MARLBORO MAN
1962

Sunday mornings at eight years old, one of my favorite things was sitting in my Doctor Dentons on the piano bench next to father, swinging my legs back and forth, feeling the vibration running through my body as the hammers hit the strings inside the piano, the constant smell of cigarettes and coffee, listening to him play Mozart, Chopin, or one of his own compositions on our piano. A piano that had belonged to my mother as a child and given to them sometime before their wedding day. I can still hear my mother's bullshit as if it was yesterday. "Hurry up, Howie. We have to pick up my folks on the way to your parents; you know how my mother hates to wait."

Sunday dinner at my Grandma Mina's apartment was still hours away, but that didn't deter Mom, whose fear of being late drove her to nagging fits of anger. We had to dress, we had to get ready, and we had to stop what we were doing to pay attention to her bullshit. No wonder Dad smoked two packs of fucking Marlboros every day for forty-five years.

My father's music both struggled and soared. He could make our piano bend to his harmonics and then adjust the pressure on the keys by the tips of his fingers, making each note stand on its own, be it sustained or momentary. His eyes closed, he is, in his mind, adrift, soaring, drinking in the sound and harmony of the instrument he held sway over. Swept away for just an instant, that moment of what he had created to produce this release. Carrying me with him, my attachment to this man's fleeting ecstasy innately opened me to my core. I vicariously lived through his personal intimacy and love of making music. The next minute, jumping up cursing under his breath at my mother, lighting up another Marlboro and walking away, and me crash landing back to my own reality, alone on the piano bench. My father's frustration was palpable, feeling rushed by my mother's ignorance of the art of the music itself; precious created space. Not seeing the frustration at the core of his anger was deeper than the moment he was walking away from. What he wanted to do and the hollow idea that rang in his head of what he thought he had to do. Knowing what he was capable of. He was an intelligent, artistic dreamer. Fragile on some level, damaged by circumstance, he was not the macho man he pretended to be. Like so many of us, settling into the life he thought was his life, but only his parents' idea.

Not sure about the location. Either Virginia or Denver.

EIGHTY-EIGHT KEYS AND THE MARLBORO MAN • 79

My father when in his element as he got older was a tough, confident man. I love this photo. I took it as he was leaving a meeting with a department of the Navy in Norfolk, Virginia, concerning satellite dishes placed on aircraft carriers. He worked for Thompson Electronic at the time as an electrical engineer. He is fifty-six years old.

Denver, Colorado, 1990. In between bouts of cancer, my father in his happy place. Grilling in his backyard for his family.

LITTLE BOAT, BIG OCEAN
1964

I was ten years old. My father gently woke me in what seemed like the middle of the night.

"Stevie, come on, kiddo, get up, go wash up, and brush your teeth. I have a surprise for you."

We dressed in the dark and drove on the Belt Parkway to Sheepshead Bay as the sun rose over Brooklyn, in route to catch one of the party boats for a day of fishing three miles offshore. The day started in a diner across the street from the pier where all the ships docked. It was full of men, together, smoking and eating. The place smelled of coffee and eggs, cigarettes, and fish. The muffled clacking of dishes and coffee cups. It was the first time I'd ever enjoyed the comfort of eggs over easy with home fries, toast with butter, and a hot chocolate.

We boarded and got the bait ready as the boat backed out of the harbor and the sun spread its light and heat over the water. The motors made soft bubbling sounds under the surface of the water as we left the land behind us. The smell of diesel fuel mixing with the sound of seagulls that circled the boat and the laughter of grown men. The ice of anticipation and fear in my belly. My father would explain what was running that day and the best way to catch it as he helped me put on my life jacket. He would bait my hook the first time, then it was up to me. "Just have fun, kiddo, and try not to get seasick."

How could I ever have imagined telling him about my secret world of mental, physical pain, and abuse at the hands of my mother, his wife? There were times those early Saturday mornings in the car or at the diner when I just wanted to jump up, cry, and scream. Letting him know that the woman he slept next to was to me a monster. He was a good man trying his whole life to be a better one. He loved his family. I miss him these days more than ever. I feel his presence; his spirit is with me as I write and live in and with this book, surrounding myself with the book, photos, music, and artifacts of my past. At times, both blessing and curse. I'm content that I never told the man anything about the situation at home. It would have killed him more quickly than the cancer finally did. I distinctly remember my initial impression, even at ten years old as we drifted and trawled three miles offshore, chasing fish, with no land in sight. Little boat, big ocean. I still get that feeling sometimes, little boat, big ocean... little boat, big ocean.

TRUMPETS, ICONS, AND FLYING SAUCERS
1970

My father was an electrical engineer of sorts, opening three successful TV repair shops in the early 1970s. His shops repaired everything from transistor radios to dishwashers. Saturdays I would take the subway from the Lower East Side to Metropolitan Avenue in Queens to "the shop" and watch my father and his men repairing huge color TVs, record players, and clock radios, air conditioners, cassette players, and eight-tracks. My father had built long, deep, carpeted workbenches for his men to work on their repairs. Each man had a station where he kept his tools and supplies. Smoking, cursing, and sharing jokes. Just being guys. Still to this day (sans the cigarettes), I love that type of workshop environment.

I remember that day being hot. Both the front and back doors of the shop were wide open with all the fans on. The only AC was where I was in my dad's office. I could sit at his desk and watch the beat of the shop through a huge picture window. Sometimes on days like these, when the shop closed for lunch, Dad and I would walk the four blocks down Metropolitan Avenue to the corner of 71st Avenue to sit in the air conditioning at Carvel and eat Flying Saucers (large flat chocolate cookies with vanilla or chocolate ice cream in the middle).

This time we climbed in his truck, a red Ford Econoline. It had "TV Repair and Electronics" in bold yellow lettering stenciled on its sides and back doors with the phone number and address. "Hey, kiddo, we can stop for ice cream on the way back. Come with me for this home repair." These were our times, intimate and lasting. He would take me from time to time just to talk.

We drove off and ended up forty minutes later in front of a humble, unassuming red brick home in Corona, Queens. I remember being greeted by a remarkably handsome, well-dressed black woman with a sweet smile and warm welcome. There was a graying Dachshund named Trumpet dancing around under foot, wagging his tail and barking.

I will never forget his voice, "Here, boy, come on. Let the men inside. Daddy needs his music back." Then he walked into the room, the air shifted around him to accommodate his presence. "Steven, this is Mr. Armstrong."

"Mr. Armstrong, this is my son, Steven." I stepped up to the legend, mouth hanging wide open in awe, and put out my hand. He simply stepped past my hand and slapped my back with a short hug and an invitation into his home. His voice sounded like butter-coated gravel. "Please come in, thanks for coming. Welcome to my home." He had an intelligent and rhyming way of talking, and that 1000-watt smile. "Come, Trumpet, good dog." How did he ever manage to talk, sing, or play his trumpet through that huge smile that seemed to live on his lips? Mr. Armstrong gave off an undeniable aura of confidence and love. It was so very heavy and deeply beautiful. I sat there on an overstuffed brown tufted, leather Chesterfield sofa in the middle of an amazingly decorated home, entirely designed and furnished by Mrs. Armstrong as a gift to her husband way back in 1943 when Mr. Armstrong came back from his first European tour.

Louis Armstrong and his reel-to-reel. My father took me there the day he repaired it. It was, and still is, a standout moment in my life. This is not my photo. It was taken off the internet. But that is the reel-to-reel in his studio that my dad repaired. Mr. Armstrong's home is now a museum in Corona, Queens. The reel-to-reel is still there.

This photo exemplifies the thousand-watt smile this man wore on his face all the time. Not my photo, taken off the internet.

Sitting on that sofa, drinking an iced Pepsi in *his* office, surrounded by albums and reel-to-reels of his music, photos of famous people of the day posing with Mr. Armstrong. Everyone from Ella Fitzgerald to Oscar Peterson to Count Basie. His assorted trumpets on small stands filling one corner of his studio. My father completed the repair of the larger of the two reel-to-reel machines sitting inside a massive wall unit. We listened to the original studio recording of "It's a Wonderful World," checking the rewind and fast forward to make sure the repair was complete. The icon thanked us both, shook both our hands, and wrote my father a check. As we walked toward the front door, Mr. and Mrs. Armstrong waved good-bye. Trumpet was standing in between them wagging his tail. On the way back to Carvel for ice cream, we both said nothing. My father had a check with Mr. Armstrong's signature on it. We had just shared the music of a living legend *with* a living legend. The smile on my father's face said it all, there was nothing that needed to be said. We listened to 1010 News on the truck's AM radio. It must have been ninety degrees and the truck had no AC. Who cares? Mr. Armstrong passed away a year later that following July 1971 a month before his seventy-fifth birthday. Mr. and Mrs. Armstrong's home has since been made into a museum. The sofa, reel-to-reels, photos, and trumpets still live there. I got goosebumps when I went back to the house to get the feeling of time and place and shake my memory for this book.

THE NAZIS, FREIGHT TRAINS, AND SPLIT MELONS

SUMMER, 1973

The immediate family on both sides (my mother's and father's sides) identified as Jews more culturally than religiously. Most fit every Jewish stereotype spoken behind their backs. Larry David had nothing that compared to my family's ability back then to invoke cringing and fear every time one of them opened their mouths.

Grandpa Moe was the most religious if you could call it that. He did make sure I had my Bar Mitzvah, sort of.

Thirty-five years before, the Nazis had exterminated six million Jewish men, women, and children.

The summer air inside and outside my father's TV and appliance repair shop's front door was blistering that day and there was no air. The front door was open, held back by a little wedge-shaped piece of rubber between the bottom of the door and the ground. This was my father's first, smaller shop, before moving to a place three times the size about one mile away. I was there that day, standing off to the side as usual, keeping my dad company while he repaired anything electronic that was put in front of him. He could fix almost anything. "There is always a way, Stevie."

I have that gene in me. Give me the right set of tools and I can fix almost anything.

A sweat-soaked pedestrian walked in carrying a small television. It had a smaller leather handle on top. I remember him tripping on the wedge-shaped rubber piece propped between the ground and the bottom of the door. I looked away smiling. Back then, people's discomfort gave me a laugh . . . My dad walked to the front of the shop, and they exchanged a nod by way of greeting the other. There seemed to be an issue with the way the TV was still working after my father had repaired it. I couldn't understand what the issue was, their exchange got louder and louder . . .

Then, *"The Nazis should have killed all you fucking Jews!!"*

It was like a bomb going off in the distance and you're far enough away not to get blown apart but blown back from the concussion. It was as though the universe had somehow managed to place a freight train barreling down the tracks at one hundred mph on the inside of my father's shoebox-shaped electronics repair shop. Propulsive wrath and abandon exploded from my father's eyes. It was acute. I recognized that feeling of power, and the beauty in the moment, and pure dread that came along with it right away. I had once been the protagonist, the hero kid, riding in on his Chuck Taylors, wielding his bat Excalibur. My father didn't need such an instrument. The soon to be severely injured gentleman was standing just on the other side of the waist-high counter at the front of the shoebox. TV in hand he was turning away, still grumbling something. I stepped back to let the train pass by. Grinning ear to ear like a Cheshire cat.

Four things unfolded in rapid succession, as follows. One, explosion; two, freight train; three, being blown to one side as my father literally dove headfirst over the counter like an Olympic athlete going for the gold, sweeping the man inches off the ground by his shirt collar, the TV smashing on the floor as glass exploded everywhere. And number four, the coup de gras. The man's head in my father's big ham hands covering his ears like giant flesh earmuffs, smashing the back of this guy's head against the side of the red faded

Ford Econoline van parked out front that happened to belong to my father. Screaming at the top of his lungs over and over, " I will kill you for what you said, I will kill you for what you said . . ." The blood, now appearing behind the man's head on the side of the van was only slightly darker than the red truck it kept repeatedly striking. I remember the connective sound that the bone to metal made. It was a metallic, echoing, choir of thud, thud, thud, thud, thud, thud, each time getting slower and slower as my dad's adrenalin was replaced by exhaustion and reality. By the time the cops and the ambulance came and pulled my father off him, the guy's head looked like a split melon. I was never so proud. He didn't have a bat, he had improvised and used the side of his truck. What a guy . . .

JEWISH COWBOYS

1989

"Look at me, son. I'm a Jewish cowboy."
"Shit, Dad, are you really going to wear that outside!?" I was completely impressed by his balance of chutzpah and cowboy panache. Dad was dressed in a red plaid shirt with mother of pearl buttons, unfastened down to the middle of his chest. A black, wide-brimmed cowboy hat and three-tone leather cowboy boots. A huge gold Jewish star on a thick gold chain hung around his neck, perfectly placed between his open shirt, nestled in his chest hair. His boot-cut jeans held up by a thick leather belt sporting an American eagle belt buckle. He had grown a thick handlebar mustache

Denver, Colorado, 1992. The Jewish Cowboy.

and long, broad sideburns. He was rockin' the look. He had become an accomplished private pilot, planned to write his memoir, as he finally discovered respect for his own life.

DEATH, DIRT, AND GOOD-BYES
1998

My father had embraced who he was by the time he died of cancer at sixty-eight years old. He had been called out of retirement and back to a division of RCA based out of Denver, Colorado, to help design the first satellite dish for home television. Being a pilot, he was able to fly around the country in a small, single-engine plane, lecturing and introducing this new technology to the country. He had started writing and playing music once again. Ironically, he talked of writing a book about his life. Authoring this part of my book, while enduring and conquering cancer of my own at the same age he died, was more than a bit freaky.

JULY 2, 1998

Two EMS technicians came and carried my father's body down the steps from the second-floor master bedroom, encased in a black vinyl zippered bag, the day that the cancer finally completed sucking him dry. I remember a wisp of his dulled, grey hair caught in the zipper. *How careless,* I thought. I stood on the top of the stairs with my hands over my ears, sobbing, shaking my head back and forth. Not believing.

Bright pea green and canary yellow chintz fabrics covered the walls and bed, white wicker furniture, scalloped eyelet throw pillows and yellow shag carpet. My parents' bedroom. My mother, sister Julie, and a hospice nurse whose name was Ann, and myself, lovingly helped my father, Howard Borodkin, cross over in the end and leave the pain of his life behind. Stationed around the bed like sentinels guarding the last decaying bits that were once my dear father.

I remember the firm, rounded leaves of the Aspen[*] trees outside the window, the sound of them clapping together in the Denver breeze, as if applauding his final performance, watching him take his last shallow, *"let me die"* breath. Watching as his mouth went pitch black as his soul lifted out of his body.

Death had taken my friend from me. I had no love or empathy for neither my mother, my sister, nor anyone else. So wrapped up in my seemingly valid narcissistic victimhood, I couldn't see anything else but my own suffering.

After EMS and the police left, the house settled into itself, clouded with a death fog as if in mourning itself. Walking down the first-floor hallway to its end, I crossed over into his office, which still held a part of him. A huge, black leather chair waited behind his desk, still showing the weighted impression of his just past existence in its seat. I sat down in the well of it, his past, flipped on his computer, opened Word, and began to write his eulogy. I never saved a copy, and God only knows what I wrote. But I do remember the opening eight words, "Our dad was many things to different people . . ."

Darkness put the day out like a cigarette under its foot. In my mother's mausoleum home, the three who he left behind sheltered, arm and arm, in the cavernous tear-filled embrace of its abyss.

---

[*] *Aspen leaves "clap in the wind" due to how the leaves are structured and pivot in the wind, making a fluttering or clapping sound.*

Bound in stark and extreme loss of the only thing that had ever held the three of us together. We knew that this was the first and final time for such an intimate, candid expression. At the cemetery, family and unfamiliar faces took turns shoveling dirt on his coffin. I finished burying him myself, not letting anyone else help, until the grave diggers completed the job with a small tractor. I spent a week in a hell they call Shiva* with more unfamiliar faces, delicately stuffing their mouths with the food that they had brought, talking quietly to each other about my dad, each trying to fill in the blanks as the other told their tale. In the center of it all, my mother and my sister sitting together on wooden chairs, red-eyed, dressed in black, all the mirrors carelessly covered with sheets. I finally freed myself, rising from the self-induced, muddled grief that death leaves behind, escaping in a cab to the airport. I flew back to New York. I spoke to my mother all of three times over the next sixteen years.

We grew up together through the 1960s, Dad loving me as best he could, learning to be an adult and father simultaneously while I learned to be a child survivor. Symptomatic of that era for both the men and women of that day, their roles as husband and wife, male and female, already defined. Void of joy, trying in love, the idea drummed into your head that your sole ambition as a man was to get your wife pregnant, work at a job that you didn't like, and find a little space for yourself at the same time. My father bought into it with his head but never in his heart. Consequently, he kept moving from one career to the next, sometimes driving a cab at night.

He developed a habit of locking himself in their bedroom where he would build shortwave radios and weird electrical meters on his workbench in the corner of the room. The meters were encased in heavy green steel boxes. Orange tubes that lit their insides. You could hear the low, soft hum the tubes gave off from the current that ran

---

* *Shiva is a time referred to as sitting shiva. Its primary purpose is to provide a spiritual and emotional healing where mourners join together. A person sits shiva for a family member.*

through them if you stood close enough. I remember turning the knobs and playing with the wavy green lines dancing across the porthole screens. "Stevie, please stop touching the buttons, kiddo!" Frantically trying to remember and duplicate the original patterns, giggling. "OK, Dad." Imagining but not really knowing if we had a shared mutual discomfort. Could he build a time machine to transport Mom back to primordial times? I was a kid, and anything was still possible until someone said no. Then you simply tried and asked again.

(1) Our Dad was many things to different people — A Son, A brother, A Husband, A father, A Grandfather, our AN UNCLE. dad was always there, He always had the answer, He always could tell you the way to Go —

He was my John Wayne, my hero

THE strength that Both my parents showed us during these last months, then weeks, and then days always set a standard for me to Gauge my strength —

My Father will be missed, But the Living are left behind to live and laugh in his memory — In the end He was reduced to a shadow, BeFore He died a whisper, a remnant of the man he was. I asked him if he still dreamed when he slept he looked at me and smiled —

He Gave me his Ring, So yes he wore it and fifty years shall I. The substance is heavier than the will ever weigh Ring, But

Original draft of eulogy, written at my father's desk.

GRANDPA MOE

Grandpa Moe . . . My Peter Pan. My best buddy who took me almost every Saturday on every one of my greatest New York City adventures of my early childhood,. It's his fault that I fell in love with the island – Manhattan, my NYC, and raised a family there.

My Grandpa Moe was a dear, playful, and beautiful man. That in all the best ways, like me, his beloved grandson, to this day at the age of seventy never grew up. They say you must connect with your inner child. His never left my side, nor mine. Again, his fault.

Thank you for letting me share this one with you . . .

The Author

OLD SPICE AND POP-TARTS SUMMER

SUMMER, 1962

G randpa Moe . . . who always dressed to the nines in some sharp colored suit and tie. My Peter Pan. He took me on the greatest normal adventures of my early childhood. A dear, playful, and beautiful man that in the best ways, like me, his beloved grandson, never grew up.

This Saturday morning Grandpa wasn't wearing his sober Saturday Sabbath suit. Instead, he was dressed in his pale blue linen sports jacket, a pressed and starched white shirt with a cotton tank top T-shirt underneath, of course. A lemon-yellow silk bowtie and cream-colored high waisted pleated pants with white suspenders. A bright white monogrammed pocket square in his jacket pocket. The whole thing was topped off by a straw hat with a yellow band to match his tie. In his cream-colored woven cloth shoes and white socks, he represented the dapper fashion of a successful, middle-aged Jewish man of the early 1960s. He stood five feet six inches tall head to toe. My hero.

Our little game, on my Saturday morning sleepovers, was my

favorite part of our weekends together. I would pretend to be asleep when he came in to wake me. He would slowly swing the door open, tiptoeing across the polished wood floors. The smell of his Old Spice entering the room minutes ahead of his footsteps. The crispness of his blue linen suit was a gentle brush against my arm as he leaned forward, brushed back my hair, and gave me little kisses on my forehead.

This morning, without pause, he rights himself, speaking in conspiratorial tones and says, "Wake up, partner, time to fly. We are going to Manhattan." The somewhat husky sound of my grandfather's voice, the excitement laced into each word, to me, sounded like the beckoning, sweet whispers of freedom. Yet undefined.

I rocketed out of bed, screaming all the way down the hall to the bathroom at the other end in a combination of half-ass cartwheels, tailspins, trips, bumps, and laughter. Grandpa walking behind me smiling, eyes twinkling, satisfied, and excited by nothing more than his grandson's complete joy.

Bathed, groomed, and brushed, it is now barely 8:45 in the morning. Grandpa and I gracefully raced downstairs to the kitchen as fast as we could in our dress clothes. There was my grandmother, fully dressed, top to bottom for Saturday services, waiting for us. Grandma looked amazing. And she was sincerely pissed, standing there in disbelief, knowing it would be her, her sister Jenny, and her sister's husband, my uncle Bernie, going to temple without us . . . once again.

Standing next to my grandmother was Leeze, laughing to herself, softly shaking her head from side to side, not saying a word. Our Leeze, as we all called her, was for the past decade my grandmother's confidant and only friend. My grandfather had hired someone else to help keep the house running. Our beloved Leeze, hired thirty years ago when she was a young woman as their housekeeper, then turning into chef and able ambassador to everyone who passed through the doors into her home . . . and it was her home. She came six days a week, 8:30 every morning and left at 5:45 every evening.

Then always went home to her family. Taking Sundays off for church.

A red-checkered tablecloth covered a breakfast table full of pancakes, toast, and eggs that sat there waiting for us as we downed two cold chocolate Pop Tarts out of the box with a glass of ice-cold chocolate milk. Mimicking my grandfather, leaning forward as we ate and drank, careful not to spill a drop of anything on our clothes. I walked through the front door outside wearing a blue seersucker suit, white shirt, tank top T-shirt underneath, blue bowtie, white belt, clean white socks lining my Buster Browns, and a grin that hurt my face from smiling so hard. We hit the street. The coolness of the early summer morning had quickly exchanged places with the oncoming press of summer heat. We walked with purpose through the well-kept Jewish community full of families strolling to Saturday services. We waved "good morning," wishing good Shabbos to what seemed like eight million people in Hebrew and English We headed toward the subway. Finally, the steps, and we ascended holding hands.

The New York subway system in the 1960s was an airless labyrinth of bare bulbs, depressing shades of gray monotone, and dirt. It was summer subway still. The world carried on above you. We stood, still holding hands as we waited for the F train to take us from Continental Avenue in Queens to Avenue of the Americas, or 6th Avenue and 50th Street to Rockefeller Center in Manhattan.

Well-dressed men, women, and children were melting like warm candles on the gray concrete platform. Then you felt the welcomed whisper of wind being chased through the tunnel by the oncoming train growing stronger. The train stormed into the station, wheels squealing out their protest as it pulled in, bringing the train to an abrupt and unglamorous stop. Everyone in the train spontaneously tilted forward, then seemed to pop back to a complete vertical position in unison. On the platform, men in suits held their hats and stepped back. The woman holding down their summer dresses and their children's hands.

"Sit down. Stevie darling, It's ten stops away. We have time till we get to the city, sweetheart. It's too hot to jump around."

We sat down on warmed, woven wicker seats. Opposite each other on each side of the car. Above our heads, porcelain covered fan blades slowly rotated, spreading the stale steel stench-around the car with its labored wind. As well as the newspapers left behind on the seats. Each car was illuminated by bare, frosted bulbs, screwed into exposed sockets, placed in small metal cages spaced across the ceiling in between the fans. Subway windows only opened from the top down to make it more difficult to jump or fall out. They were all open. The doors were also drawn back on either end of each car. The sound cacophonous and clashing, pushing up against your senses like a thousand swords and shields knocking against each other in battle. There was a constant accompaniment of blaring, high-pitch squeals and whistles every time the spinning metal wheels slipped and moved against the inertia and swaying of the coupled cars, moving at thirty-five miles an hour, snaking and twisting through the tunnel. If you leaned forward in your seat, you could see into the other cars, watching all the other people in their seats or standing. Seeing from one end of the train to the other. I sat there in my blue seersucker suit of sweat and cool. Staring at the announcements of the Miss Subway winners, mixed in among all the cigarette ads. Anything Grandpa had to say to me was communicated in a sign-language type of movement with his hands, combined with over exaggerated movements of his lips to make sure I understood what he was trying to say. I would simply nod my head in response or give him an okay sign to let him know I got it. The wind that blew through the cars had a metallic weight to it. It spoke to me about adventure, new and unexplored places. The feeling that anything can happen, that anything is possible.

Finally, we arrived at Radio City Music Hall, one of our favorite haunts. Air conditioning, upholstered burgundy-colored, velvet front row seats. I remember everyone that worked there, wearing red, bellhop style uniforms with shiny black shoes and red caps.

Those amazing Rockettes, Grandpa and I sharing a large bucket of popcorn with extra butter, and a Coke with two straws. Watching a short newsreel, cartoons, and our favorite thing, the previews. My grandpa, saying after each one, "We'll have to come back to see that one. Right, Stevie?" Then a box of Bon Bons and the feature film. Those days were magic.

THE WHITE WHALE AND THE BAR MITZVAH BOY
NOVEMBER, 1966

At twelve, I was sent off to Sunday School at Mount Sinai Temple in Forest Hills for my Bar Mitzvah lessons. Instead, I would take the subway for fifteen cents three stops more to my Grandpa Moe's apartment in Forest Hills on 67th Avenue. My grandfather had sold their house and moved himself and Grandma Ruth into an apartment in the same neighborhood.

There was no need for the empty space feeling in the house since both his daughters, my Aunt Ellen and my mother, were both married. The vestibule had a panel of buzzers lined up in four columns, The names placed in alphabetical order with the corresponding apartment number to the left, on a piece of black plastic labeling strips, with white lettering. To the left of that was a little black button.

RAHMEY – 2H

There was never any need to press the button. People just let me in. My grandparents lived on the second floor, so I never had to wait for the elevator. Instead, I took the steps two at a time, one flight up and made a left to their door, which was always already open for me. Grandpa would be cooking one of his favorite omelets. Which basically was any leftovers in the refrigerator less than a week old that mixed or didn't mix well with five or six eggs in Grandma Ruth's cast iron frying pan. After we ate and cleaned up, I would follow him into the living room and sit at my grandfather's feet surrounded by the smell of polished furniture and assumed wealth. My breath still smelling like the eggs we had just consumed. Sitting on the soft imported Asian carpets (called oriental rugs back then), my head on his lap, his perfectly pleated slacks my pillow, his free hand placed softly in my hair stroking the top of my head. He never once asked me why I didn't want to go to Sunday School for my Hebrew and bar mitzvah lessons. It was a "don't ask, don't tell" kind of thing. Me knowing it would be ok that I was here with him, that he would take care of it. The message passed between two friends, together immersed in classic literature and poetry. Letting time pass by chapter and verse, not seconds and minutes. I still read and write that way. No minutes, no seconds, only words.

He also knew I had more going on at home than I shared. Not once did he ask. Not once did I volunteer any inkling of the horror. In hindsight we both fucked that up. Grandpa Moe gave me a safe place, free of prying and bribing to get me to talk. Instead, I sat listening to him read me Dickens, Emmerson, *Alice in Wonderland*, and Melville's *Moby Dick*. He would read me the story of Pinocchio in Italian . . . I'll never forget the opening line of that book: "Ciera ulna volta un bambino che si e' fatto di legno." ("There once was a little boy who was made of wood.") No shit.

The big day, finally my bar mitzvah had arrived. My grandfather had the rabbi print the Hebrew symbols in English for all the passages I needed to read on small pieces of paper and place them in the appropriate spots marked off on each page of the Torah. I did exactly what I was told to do. We all did what needed to be done. The plan went off without a hitch. Everyone was relieved. To this day, I am convinced that my grandfather made the rabbi a deal he could not refuse based on some sort of blackmail, I mean business deal. Which seems to have been Grandpa Moe's thing. It was most likely the horses or dice at the fire house. But somehow, I couldn't see the rabbi bending over behind the fire trucks rolling dice.

No one ever found out. That is, until I published this book. Besides, they're all dead anyway.

I received about six thousand dollars for my bar mitzvah, which wasn't a bad haul back then. My parents must have cleared close to five grand in profit. Which, in retrospect, could have been one of the reasons for having my bar mitzvah in the first place. The hot coffee and cheap-ass cold buffet I remember avoiding was laid out on large, round, clear plastic plates, covered in beds of quickly wilting, dark, green ruffled lettuce. Each one holding pathetic mounds of cream-cheese, sliced onions, and tomatoes. And of course the center piece with an extra bed of lettuce placed on some type of pedestal and smoked salmon (or lox, as we Jews call it). It was laid out on a long table draped in a clean tablecloth, displaying almost washed-out stains between the dishes of food. Back then this had to be five-hundred-dollars, tops. They finally broke down and bought me a black and white six string electric guitar and small amplifier. Which was, admittedly, outstanding. I had hours of fun learning to make music and playing. Trying to play along to my Beatles records. The experience of owning and playing an instrument had that lasting, overwhelming, and combined effect that only freedom of self-expression and sound brings. I can honestly say it was one of the only gifts I remember them buying me, except for the bat.

DRIVER OF THE CHOSEN PEOPLE

NOVEMBER, 1972

David Bowie reveals his stunning alter ego Ziggy Stardust and changes the way we see and hear music forever, also blowing my mind. Pong becomes the first commercial successful video game and alters our way of seeing media, entertainment, and the world.

I had just turned eighteen four months before, studied, then applied for my driver's license. My father taught me how to drive, using the 1970 eight-cylinder, blue and white, two-door Chevy Impala convertible that his dad, my Grandpa Abe, bought for us. The family car. Bluntly stated, it was fuckin' kick ass and smoking hot. Especially with the top down.

Unfortunately, I never got to enjoy the opportunity to drive it myself, which would have most definitely ended in disaster. The ineptly stupid, splintered, unsurvivable life I was up to my neck in at the time would have guaranteed that debacle. Most likely ending in a cinematic high-speed fiery crash off a bridge, cruising with the top down and no seat belts in sight, at ninety miles an hour, listening to Led Zeppelin on one of my eight tracks, smoking a joint. Flying through the air and the windshield, so stoned, never feeling my face and skull melt away from the impact. A writer's mind . . . News at eleven. "Let's go to the video tape."

Interestingly enough though, to take my driving test, I used my Grandpa Moe's four-door, mucus brown, Rambler America Ambassador. He had insisted to my father that this titanic-sized machine was a better choice than a much smaller, easier to handle sports car. I knew Grandpa Moe had his reasons. He never did anything without having the next and final move in place. I knew instinctively that his master plan involved my unwavering help. Another Peter Pan adventure with my childhood hero.

My grandfather had remained my closest and most trusted ally the last four years. We had dinner and spoke on the phone all the time. He vehemently opposed my choice and my fabricated reasoning for my lifestyle and place of residence and made sure he voiced his love and concern every time we spoke.

How could I ever tell him what his daughter was, what his daughter did, and expect him to carry on with his life? Imagine him knowing what I so deliberately denied him from learning. I cannot begin to imagine the consequences, the tsunami it would create. Wiping out every family member in its wake. Would they blame me?

It was my ominous, childhood duty to make sure that I would take my own life before ever voluntarily speaking up or admitting to it to anyone who might one day happen to ask if there was anything wrong between me and mommy dearest.

I adhered to and maintained this disciplined protocol most of my adult life, until I started writing this book.

When I was eighteen years old, some ten years later, the places on my body the monster had touched would still cry out in pain, with no way for me to control it. I would find myself sitting in a dark bathroom with the door closed, rocking back and forth, moaning in pain and loneliness. I cried all the time in private. My anger is the only gift I can remember my mother ever giving me. I paid that gift forward, and I handed out presents to anyone that I decided I didn't like and beat the shit out of anyone that got in my way. I had become my own monster. Anger, the gift that keeps on giving.

Through years of outstanding therapy, developed spiritual and self-awareness, and the innate drive, propelling me to absorb, learn, and read as much as I could, I have more than just survived. I have thrived in all ways. It is much easier and more fun to love than to hate. Especially oneself. Love is all there is.

I digress . . . Saturday morning. I'm in position, motor running, like the driver in a bank heist, sitting behind the wheel of Grandpa's car stationed by the service entrance behind Temple Sinai on Ascan Avenue, in Forest Hills, Queens. This was only on the weekends Grandma Ruth was in Brooklyn with my Aunt Ellen, their younger daughter.

Grandpa and I had placed small strips of electric tape in their driveway, directly in front of both front tires, where the car was supposed to be parked until Sunday morning. I had learned this trick from Senior. When we returned the car, we could roll it up to the exact spot it was when my grandmother had been home and remove the tape before she saw it. She knew Moe, and she knew us as a team. She didn't trust either one of us. We both knew she had her own way of checking to see if we used the car on the Sabbath when she was away. To this day I never understood why she never simply checked the milage.

Moe had devised a plan. He, Martin (Marty) Eisenberg, and Harry Zarin would attend the Saturday services at the temple as usual. After the service, it was prearranged that the three Jewish amigos would quietly duck out the back door to their designated driver. This driver would safely, expertly speed them through the Midtown Tunnel, then east on the Cross-Island Parkway to Aqueduct Racetrack for an afternoon of beer, cigars, and betting on the horses. That was me, yours truly. Driver of the chosen people.

These three hard-working Jewish gentleman, family men indeed, needed a simple timeout. Not being able to drive themselves on the Sabbath, they enlisted my help, Grandpa Moe was a fucking genius. We made several trips, but not many. Each was special. One of my fondest memories from that misbegotten time in my life is the safety and cradling comfort that their warm timbre of their baritone voices portrayed as they zigzagged between English and Yiddish as they prayed and planned and assuredly thanked God for me. Then covering their yarmulkes with baseball caps. The car's interior was blanketed with cherry tobacco smoldering in their beautifully hand-crafted pipes.

The firstborn of immigrant parents, now with their own children and grandchildren. They had successful businesses and loved God. They were the grown children of those who escaped the Nazi death, carrying numbers on their forearms. And dreams of freedom and hope for their families in their hearts. I don't know what they told their wives about where they disappeared to on Saturday afternoons. It didn't really matter. They each gave me ten bucks to keep my mouth shut.

Always from the back of the car,
"Stevie, I love you, boy."
"Yes grandpa."
"Stevie, remember this, loose lips sink ships."
"Yes, sir. I'll remember, and I love you back."

Laughing to myself. Living on the streets with Senior, Tony, and the gang. My mouth had its own zipper on it. I was capable of completely forgetting anything I wasn't supposed to hear and forgetting anything I wasn't supposed to know. Guilty by association.

The four of us, without fail, always ended up at Sammy's Romanian on Forsyth Street. Plates of homemade chicken liver and schmaltz, pickles and potato pancakes, Romanian steak and vodka encased in blocks of ice, wrapped in dishtowels. We ate and drank to closing. I walked the four blocks back to my flat. Sammy's was in the hood. I loved watching the Rambler's taillights fade as my grandfather and his friends somehow drove down Delancey Street and over the Williamsburg Bridge back to Queens.

UNINTENDED GOOD-BYES, PANCAKES, AND GLYCERIN TABLETS
1974

Richard Nixon becomes the first United States president forced to resign from the Oval Office after the Watergate scandal. Muhammad Ali knocks out George Foreman in the eighth round in a match held in Zaire called the Rumble in The Jungle. I thought that both were of parallel significance and fit together nicely since both were knockouts.

The T-Bone Diner, 107-48 Queens Boulevard. It first opened in 1934, and over the past thirty years it had chiseled out a solid and proud history of serving the best food with a smile to everyone who walked through its hallowed doors. The first-time Grandpa brought me to *"The Bone,"* as it was affectionately called by those in the know, was in 1962 for breakfast. We were both a lot younger back then . . . Funny that fourteen years later, we still had that reflected twinkle in each other's eyes, that arc of energy as we sat there facing each other. God, how I loved, and still to this day, love this man. Grandpa would always make sure I walked in ahead of him. The warm, gentle, guiding grip of his hands on my shoulders as he helped me push the door open. Protecting me, making sure I was always in plain sight where he could see me, touch me. I loved the touching and affection with no strings attached. As we passed through the same hallowed entryway with the doors still pushing against our backs, closing behind us, "Good morning, Mr. Rahmey, good morning, Stevie boy!" Scurrying past us, around us, as if on roller skates. In and out of the kitchen through the constantly swinging In & Out doors. To and from the tables and booths. "So good to see you." *Zooooom!!* Balancing plates somehow, walking and talking, "You both look very sharp this morning, the usual?" *Zooooom!!*

The diner was our place. A secret for the two of us to plan our day together and to pig-out on diner food. Plates of triple-stacked buttermilk pancakes overpowering the plates that they were served on, smothered in real maple syrup and melted butter. Slices of thick cut bacon tucked in between each pancake. Always my grandfather's Kellogg's Corn Flakes in warm water, black coffee with honey, served with everything he ate for breakfast. Why warm water and not milk for his cereal and black coffee with honey? According to my grandfather, putting honey in your coffee made the day sweeter. I asked a dozen times, "Why the water and not milk, Grandpa?" and never got a straight answer. What I believe is that growing up, his family never had enough money to buy milk all the time, so they made do without it. To this day I still drink my coffee black with honey. He was right, it absolutely makes every day a little sweeter, even with the crap that gets hurled at you as an adult.

We went to the Bone every Saturday morning that we got to spent together after the Saturday Sabot services or on our way to Manhattan. We always sat at "our booth." If there was some other family sitting and enjoying their breakfast in our booth, we would wait for that table even though the rest of the diner was empty. Grandpa would order a coffee, me a large chocolate milk, and we'd wait at the counter, sitting on big, round, green upholstered stools bolted into the floor that spun around super-fast until it made you dizzy. Sipping his, bottomless cup of black coffee, he would *kibbitz** with all the waiters in Yiddish. I didn't understand what they were saying, but it looked like from there smiles, laughter, and body language it was for grownups only.

When we were seated, they would ask us how our families were by name and Grandpa would ask the same of them. Weddings, deaths, new babies, they always bantered about the word *meshuga*† always followed closely by some one's name. "*Herbie? Oy, vhat a meshuga!*"

At twenty years old, I'm glued to my seat in horror, wondering how in the hell I'm going to tell my sweet, conniving, gentle man, my best friend, I was going away. I sat there, a big mug of hot chocolate warming my hands, watching him, studying him. For what seemed like hours but are only minutes.

Older. White shirt, white cotton tee underneath, soft gold suit and tie, hat, and pocket square, polished wingtips. Sitting on the edge of his seat, his posture composed and youthful. His love of life showing in everything he did. Secret maps, winding paths to Neverland, and trails through dark woods and city streets to new and better days. All this still dancing in his head, playing on his lips. His unabashed, hypnotic charisma shining through.

We stood up and put our coats on, leaving cash on top of the table without a bill, including a nice tip. Standing outside in front of the diner, we hugged good-bye, kissing each other's faces, embracing over and over. My face buried in his neck, soaking in the Old Spice and the memories of innocent times its scent invoked. As he kissed my ear for what was to be the final time, he whispered, "Come on Stevie, let's go play again like we used to." I raised my head off the soft, clean surface of his physical presence, shook out

---

* Kibbitz, a verb. To kibbitz means to stand around talking and making wisecracks.
† Meshuga or meshuganer is the surname given to someone who is completely off the hook, bat-shit crazy. It is not to be taken lightly.

my internal self, and heavily, whispered back, "I've done terrible things, Grandpa, and I have to go far away for a while."

"I know, my love. I see it in your eyes. The light has gone out of them. They are dark and full of pain, old pain . . . I'm not sure why, Stevie. I will be here when you are ready to come home, then we can go and play again." Leaning back away from the hug, he stared directly into my eye. My love allowing him to enter, me able to hide the decades of pain and the shame of my childhood. Proud of myself that he would never know. His joy uncorrupted by his daughter's corrupt and rotting soul and the torturous undoing of his grandson at her hand. "Stay safe, no matter what you do, and don't forget to come back to me, my love."

I never saw him again. He fell to the floor from a heart attack a month after I left in his bedroom, putting on crimson red striped socks, while I was living in Canada, still running in circles, trying to run away from myself. He died alone, my grandmother walked in and found him there, half-dressed I suppose. His suit still laid out on the bed, now forever, or until they buried him in it, I suppose. In reflection, I feel more than a little responsible for his death, not being there, and all.

My mother told the family after he needlessly died that he suffered with angina and never told anyone but her, his trusted, eldest, daughter. The glycerin tablets he was supposed to take, he never did. He had told my mother they were a pain in the ass to remember to take and it did not matter anyway. He'd be simply fine and to please not tell the rest of the family, especially Stevie. Like my fucking mother would have told me anyway.

My Grandpa Moe was a wise-ass, poet. Peter Pan, mentor, and one hell of a salesman to the very end. He could sell ice to the Eskimos.

Sometimes you have had enough, leaving your fate and faith to the wind and the hand of God. Feeling the weight of the final realization that it might be closing time. My grandpa, Moe Rahmey, had the gift and simple blessing of knowing the Universe was telling him it was okay to leave. That God knew he had done the best he could have done his whole life for his family and that it was an appropriate time to check out. To close his eyes and rest with no 6:30 wakeup call ever again.

GRANDPA ABE

Not sure of the location or who took the photo. Looks like the late 1950s, early 1960s. Abraham Borodkin was a poet, lyricist, artist, composer, master of four languages and self-expression, and my buddy. Grandpa Abe, with his ever-present pipe. His spirit runs deep in my bones.

Grandpa Abe, my dad's father. Dressed in a white shirt open at the neck, suspenders, and brown slacks. Always with a pipe, notepad, and pencil. Writing something down in his ever-present notebook. Never looking up until I said, "Hey, Grandpa." This man became an unconditional counterweight to the darkness and depravity I experienced at home all of the time.

LOVE AND THE CREATIVE MIND
1961

At six years old my weekend sleepovers at my grandparents were incredibly special. Sunday mornings, I would wander into their dining room. My grandfather used the space for his studio. I was drawn at times by the sound of my grandfather's cello or his humming as he stroked the keys on their baby grand piano. There he sat, pencil behind one ear, pipe in his mouth, bouncing up and down every time he had an idea and bit down. Spilling the ashes on his pants and all over the piano he was sitting in front of, which pissed off my grandmother to no end. Grandpa's sheet music, pencils, pens, and more ashes from his pipe were already sprinkled across the dining room table.

Grandma Mina would be in her kitchen cooking that evening's dinner, chopping, dicing, and humming, listening to Mozart or Brahms on the AM radio that made its home on top of the refrigerator. Always tuned to WQXR, the only classical music station on the dial.

"Abe, *please* be careful with your ashes by the piano, and I hope you already put the table pads on to cover the table. You know it scratches."

The dining room table was my grandmother's most prized possession. It was the table her beloved family gathered around every Sunday. It was her wooden pride and joy.

My Grandmother Mina was also a musician and a piano teacher for most of her life. She taught me and all the kids in the neighborhood to play the piano, read notes, and write music. Then their children, then the grandchildren. When she was in her late nineties, still teaching, she sat me down one day when we were alone and told me, "You were one of the most gifted and worst students that I ever tried to give instruction to. You were just an awful little boy to deal with, Stevie."

Smiling, opening her arms, drawing me in for a hug.

"But you are my first grandchild, and I'm so proud of you." Still laughing, she asked, "Do you remember *anything* I taught you?"

When my grandfather started to play one of his pieces, Grandma Mina would always stop what she was doing and come into the dining room, wiping her hands on the apron that seemed to be permanently tied around her waist. My Aunt Sue would wander out of her bedroom, taking a break from her homework when she heard the first few familiar notes. There we would sit on my grandmother's blue damask sofa, three of us together hand in hand, me in the middle, thrilled as my grandfather proudly played one of the new pieces for his family on their piano.

Sometimes he would play his cello. His right hand delicately held the bow as the strings danced and sang, responding like a lover to his touch as his left hand caressed the neck of his instrument in perfect step with the bow. He would sway back and forth, sometimes with his eyes closed, then abruptly stop to change a note or the tempo of what he had just heard himself play.

LOVE AND THE CREATIVE MIND • 121

Grandma Mina at 98 years old playing the family piano. When she died, my cousin Marnie had the piano moved to California to her home, where it sits today.

My Aunt Rhona in her late 80s, 2018, playing that same piano to my newborn cousin, Zane. He would be the 4th generation to have heard it played.

He wrote and played at times for hours, till he couldn't lift his bow or pencils any longer. Me sitting there watching him the whole time. Walking over to the sofa, he would lift me on his lap with a kiss on my forehead and we would both fall asleep, my head pressed against his chest, comforted by the pace of his breathing and the scent of his pipe tobacco. The sensation of his clean pressed shirt rubbing against the side of my face. Comforted by the unmatched safety and love from this extraordinary man.

He would wake suddenly and gently lift me off his lap, jumping up. Stoking his pipe back to life till it blazed and belched like a smokestack. I still remember the sweet scent of his pipe as he lifted me off the sofa, his presence once again filling the room as he hummed what he was working on while he had been asleep. He would walk back and forth through the bluish haze of smoke he had created, pushing it into slow swirls around him, casting designs in the air, in the afternoon sun coming in through the slats of the venetian blinds.

Weekdays during the summer, we would take the bus together down Queens Boulevard to the courthouse where we would sit in the air conditioning for hours as I watched him sketching, using charcoal and pencils, drawing the jurors, attorneys, and their clients as the cases were brought before the judge. He always wore a white shirt, suspenders and a belt under a brown suit. We would walk back down Queens Boulevard, hand in hand, and stop at Jahn's, the best ice-cream parlor around, back in the day. We would sit at the counter, looking at his drawings in his small notebook and each get huge black and white ice cream sodas with whipped cream. They came with long red-and-white-striped paper straws and spoons that had really long handles. Turning sideways and looking at me, eating his ice cream laughing, he would always say, "Please don't tell your grandmother, she'll stop talking to the both of us!"

After a while, we would say it together, and end with a wink of the eye.

STAGE LEFT
FRIDAY NIGHT, JANUARY 17, 1964

I am nine years old. The opening performance of *Hello, Dolly*. I remember it being ridiculously cold and snowing like mad. I was wearing my rubber galoshes (boots) over my shoes with the pant legs of my suit tucked into the tops. As a young kid, unnoticed, I always got to wander around the theaters I went to with Grandpa. The union would call him if one of the Broadway show orchestras needed a cellist. Grandpa Abe got to play his cello in the orchestra of a lot of Broadway shows through the 1960s. I went with him to quite a few. Always seeking out the stagehands and actors. Invariably, drawn to the side of the stage where I could just see the audience up front from behind the curtains. And be as close to the production on stage as I could without getting in the way. There I could feel the glorious, choreographed, stampeding energy of the live performance.

"What a sweet little boy! What is your name?"

"Stevie. My grandpa plays in the orchestra," I stammered. "He, he plays the cello."

Staring down and smiling, she answered sweetly, "Well, you stay right there, Stevie whose grandpa plays the cello. I'll sing this next song for you."

I was immediately enthralled by that amazingly infectious smile and the touch of Carol Channing's hands on my cheeks. I had no idea who she was, but she was bright and shiny, and larger than life.

I had been to Broadway performances before to hear my grandfather play, but this was my first opening night. The theater was packed. I stood there feeling that familiar magic starting to take hold, the anticipation of the live music beginning to course through my veins as the conductor raised his baton and the orchestra went silent, holding their breath, waiting for the conductor's command. For that brief moment, collectively, instinctively, the audience holds its breath as well. Then release, feeling the sound instantly flood the theater. Feeling the rumble in my stomach from the dozens of instruments as I watch the lights go up on stage.

The depth of Mrs. Channing's voice reached in and touched my heart, just as the palm of her hand had reached down and touched my cheek moments before.

I was able to experience *Hello, Dolly* four times, standing stage left for every performance. Mrs. Channing said hello to me each night I showed up, even if it was a casual glance or a wink. The union called Grandpa Abe to another production two months later. She shook Grandpa's hand and thanked him for his contribution to the show before we left the theater for the final time.

Each one of Broadway's elaborate and extreme details gave me an undeniable feeling of freedom and energy. When I knew I was going to a weekend matinee, it didn't matter what performance it was. Who cared? I was dressed and good to go, standing by my grandfather's cello, packed in its case in his living room, thirty-minutes too early. Like a drug, I felt myself craving the sound, lights, and the unfiltered power of The Great White Way. I had no desire to participate in it, but instead, stand close enough as an observer to not miss one beat of its glorious heart.

Grandpa Abe introduced me to the conductor and all his friends in the orchestra each time we got to a new theater. We always got to walk through the side door with all the actors and other musicians. Some shows I was able to sit in the orchestra pit under the stage. Not being able to see the production at all. Even better, I got to watch the conductor elegantly guide my grandfather and his fellow musicians as they focused and swayed in time to the strokes of the conductor's baton. It was hypnotizing. A magical experience, hearing the singing and lyrics from above my head, and the profound musical accompaniment that danced all around me.

Abraham Borodkin, a Jewish Russian immigrant, who fled his homeland with my grandmother as young children, escaping the pogroms. Smuggled out of their villages on a potato cart, buried under sacks of potatoes, through dark cemeteries in the middle of the night to the shipping docks, to ships waiting to take them away from the terror of anti-Semitism for a price as they made their way with their families to Europe then to America, through Ellis Island.

Abraham was an intellect. He spoke fluently in four different languages. A consummate musician, composer, and painter, his eclectic library of musical compositions is a mix of jazz, chamber music, orchestral, and opera pieces. Through the 1950s, '60s, and '70s, a sizable amount of his work was performed regularly by other orchestras and bands for the *NBC Radio Hour*. He collaborated with Perry Como and Skitch Henderson & The Skitch Henderson Orchestra. He played at Carnegie Hall as well as the Lincoln Center. One of his greatest moments was playing on the first musical, live public radio broadcast on NPR in 1948 with the famous Springwood String Quartet.

When my dad passed away back in 1998, I took all the boxes of my grandfather's work that my father had taken when his father died. I started to make my way through the vast treasure that made up the body of his work, which included every composition he had, along with every handwritten note and all the accompanying instrumentation. Some came with the matching vinyl recording. I came upon an urban-cool recording with all his original notation for each of the twenty-five instruments. A jazzy homage, big band piece, written in the early 1940s. It is a soundful, joy-filled proclamation of his love for New York City's vibrancy and the music of that time. Dedicated to, *"My friend, George Gershwin."*

Perry Como and my grandfather at NBC Studios, 1964.

THE WEIGHT
1979

At eighty-two years old, one of the most gifted men I ever knew spent his final days sitting on the sofa the two of us shared our Sunday afternoon naps on seventeen years ago. Every five minutes, he would ask for me as though waiting for a younger version of me to reappear. He would thank me for stopping by, not knowing who I was, telling me that I seemed like a "genuinely nice young man." Cupping both his hands in both of mine, kissing them, I would reply, "It is my pleasure, Mr. Borodkin," sobbing uncontrollably as I looked into the sparkling gaze of his dark brown, vacant eyes. Those tears stain the pages of this final draft in recollection, completing this passage, as with so many others in this recalling of my life, called memoir.

The last time I saw my grandfather, he was sitting in his dining room, pencil and pad in his hands, smoking his pipe, the front of his crisp, white shirt covered in ashes, humming away. Smiling and taking copious notes about some unknown melody. Sketching and drawing landscapes and portraits of people and places in his past.

It could have been seventeen years ago, like I had stepped through a time barrier back into the past. But it wasn't. He was an old gray shell of the man he was, and I was a young man, angry, and very damaged, with a heart of gold, possessing love and empathy, blinded with a head full of pain, misery, and shame.

I've never doubted my talent or that I would make music and write during my life. I received my first six-string electric guitar when I was thirteen years old and never could do the things I wanted to do with it. I picked up my first bass guitar in 1983 and fell in love.

Joyfully, I still play and write music. In many ways, it is who I am.

As for my writing? We all think we can. Or at least thought we could, if we ever tried. When I tell people about my memoir, they always comment about wanting to do that but never having the time. In my sixties, as I sit and write word upon word, page after page for the past eight years, I say, time is all we do have. We get only one precious life. We are, each of us, unique; and trust me, we all have a story in us. Whether it is fiction or reality. So, get cracking!

It is a gift and blessing for me to be a Borodkin, humbled by the amount of unfiltered talent that cascades at times through my veins, my heart and mind. I am an artist, I am a musician, I am a poet and a learning and talented writer, and it's all your fault.

Thank you, Grandpa Abe.

BOOK THREE
BLOOD, GOD, ANGELS, AND DOGS

"The world is indeed full of frightening things, and we are helpless creatures surrounded by forces that are inexplicable and unbending. The average man, in ignorance, believes that those forces can be explained or changed, he doesn't really know how to do that, but he expects the actions of mankind will explain them or change them sooner or later.

Carlos Castaneda,
A Separate Reality

THREE LITTLE ASSHOLES
SEPTEMBER, 1974

Senior asked Jerry to bring me and Tony to the club. When I asked Tony what it was about, he shook his head, "He wants to talk to us, wise guy."

I was 20 years old and had been living on Eldridge Street for six years. I knew the drill. As expected, the club was empty. Jerry locked the door so we wouldn't be disturbed. We felt it as soon as we walked in. Senior was not sitting in his usual spot, instead pacing back and forth behind the bar, smoking, anxious to get off his chest what needed to be said. He was incredibly angry... he knew.

Senior had found out about the paid beating of some unknown creep yesterday down on Stanton Street. The guy was in the hospital in extremely critical condition.

I had come clean with Senior two years before as we sat alone in the club. I told him the whole-nine-yards, everything. I told him why I had run away, tearfully telling him the painful and disgusting things my mother had repeatedly done to me as he sat there with tears of his own. He was an extremely shrewd man; he had put two and two together.

He heard us carrying on in the club just days before about how sick people are who screw with children and how and what should be done to them. The guys kept asking aloud to no one and anyone, "Who would do those things to a little kid?"

Senior had read my body language and saw the darkness rise up in me, looking for trouble.

Then Senior opened the spigot and let the shit pour down. "*You three little assholes, including my fucking asshole of a shithead son, have deeply fucked up. Do you have ANY fucking idea what you've FUCKING done? Jesus H. Christ . . . I've heard this guy is less than dirt, a real fuckin' creep . . . We were working on a solution. I'm no friggin' idiot, but you made me look like one!! Anyone who fucks with little kids like that deserves what he got or death!*" Slamming both palms on the bar, he faced us full on.

"*But it was my mother fuckin' responsibility, God-damn it! MY FUCKING RESPONSIBILITY.*"

A tirade from a man who, in the five years I knew him, never lost his cool, never said a four-letter word in public.

Senior's anger had consumed us. Silence awkwardly settled back in. Tony had stopped breathing, placing his hands on his head, and his head in his lap. Jerry's expression looked as if he was choking on something he was eating. I sat there, mouth wide open, again about to pee my pants. He took a deep breath, downed a shot of Jack, lit a Newport, and combed his hair back into place. Calmer, he continued, "Seems this piece of horse-shit you guys seriously tuned up is very well-connected. He is the son and disgrace of a family up on Tremont Avenue in the Bronx. He had already been seen down here, hanging out by the school. Whatever, it is too late now. So, here is the deal . . . Tony is my son, needless to say he is good to go. He *will* get his fuckin' ass kicked soundly for letting you and Jerry talk him into it, and beyond that he is totally fucked for the foreseeable future. Jerry is going on a well-deserved vacation to some undisclosed location south of here for an exceptionally long time. It is you, Stevie, they want to use to even the score. The way they see it, unfortunately, you are the odd man out. I told them directly that you are a valued part of my family and crew, like a son to me. But you are not, in the end, my son." He seemed sad and upset for not being able to make things better for me, for us. He looked tired from his outburst. A bit subdued, "I did everything but beg trying to figure another way to make this right. They are not fuckin' around, kid; it will take a long time and a lot of asses kissed to make this right. I'm deeply sorry." The revealing declaration of the facts laid out before all of us rattled around in my ears a bit before sinking into my brain like a bullet. I was face-punched. Not since my days jumping tenement roofs had I felt death's door. Now, once again, its icy presence ran through my veins. A bat to someone's head was not going to solve my problems this time. I was in fucked city. Stunned, I answered, "Senior, isn't there anything you can do? What does odd fuckin' man out mean!? So now what? Do I die and life goes on?? They caught this guy with his pants down and his mouth full."

Somberly, he replied, "I hear you. It disgusts me as well, but you guys should have come to me. This guy might die from his injuries. All this will take time to sort out, which means you need to disappear for a while, a long while till we get past this. You are going to live, just not around here."

"Why can't I go with Jerry?"

Continuing mournfully, "Because it's not far enough. I have made arrangements with friends of mine. These friends have a contracting business supplying the military with medical supplies and a small amount of skilled manpower to handle the delivery to our boy over there. After some basic training, you'll fly from here in the States to over there, where the stuff is being delivered." Pointing with his thumb over his shoulder . . . in Cambodia."

Bullseye. The last blow hit home; every ounce of air had left my lungs. But he wasn't close to done yet. "Simply load up here, unload the cargo over there at the airport, and come back home. You will also get paid a sum of money, which I will personally watch over until your return. You'll be away from here, make some money, and only overseas for short periods and away from all the action. So, let us say eight months from now we will meet here again?" His eyes trying to warm against the arctic blast of reality that had just blown in. "You guys will leave first thing in the morning . . . pack a small bag of personal belongings and clothing. Leave whatever is valuable in the flat; give Tony the keys. Do you hear me, Stevie? You are a man with family waiting for you to come back . . . you got it? I will tell Jerry where he needs to take you. Tony will go with you. Don't worry, it will be okay, I'll see ya soon enough." He planted a kiss on my lips and hugged me like the father he wasn't.

"See ya when ya get back, kid."

GHOSTS AND ZOMBIES
SEPTEMBER, 1974

The Buick moved uptown toward its early morning destination. Tony, Jerry, and I were lost in what we had done and the undeniably fucked up consequences of our actions. Knowing no matter where we ended up, it would be a while till the three of us would see each other after today.

The Buick stopped on the northwest corner of 48th Street and Tenth Avenue. We sat there long enough to pass around a final joint. Ten minutes later, a white van pulled up behind us and flashed its headlights. Jerry looked at me sitting in the back through the rearview mirror, and I knew it was time to go. I took a last hit on the joint we had started, grabbed my stuff, got out, and closed the door without looking back. Expelling the smoke from my lungs just like I had done a hundred times before, this time too full of anxiety to feel the effect. The Buick pulled away. I was once again on my own. A twenty-year-old man/child.

I walked up to the passenger side of the van as the window rolled down, sinking into the door, letting clouds of cigarette smoke happily escape from inside the van's interior, free, rising into the city air like helium-filled balloons. Wishing at that moment I was able to grab on, rising above the situation at hand. Joyfully floating away with them. Higher and higher until the harsh topography below was just an indistinguishable little smudge.

The driver's voice sent me crashing to earth like Thor's Hammer.

"Kid, hey, kid, I'm Johnny B, your driver."

Shaken, I replied, "I'm Stevie."

"Come on get in, we got to move, and don't sit in the front seat."

I opened the passenger side door and climbed in through the empty front seat into the back. Smiling, Johnny B continued, "I heard you're a tough guy . . . seems there was some guy up in the Bronx whose brother was found ass up and face down under the bridge by the water at the bottom of Allen Street three days ago. His pockets empty, and all his gold teeth pulled out, a gaping hole where his balls used to be. Word on the street was that this piece of shit fucked with little girls and little boys in your neighborhood. Looks like the human waste you had tuned up will not be fucking with any kids anymore, he died last night."

I had not heard about him dying. Senior had been right to get us all out of town for a while. It was my particular destination that was a bit . . . over the top. I went numb. Expressionless, I answered, "Too bad." Thinking, *Holy shit, we really did fuck things up*. To be fair, I was still not unhappy about the outcome. The van pulled away and faded into the serpentine vehicular landscape, moving farther uptown, its tires and springs mournfully complaining, suffering the pot-holed streets toward the George Washington Bridge on 175th Street, I imagined. I had never been that far north; it was the only place of which I could think. Daylight cast stark and strobe-like flashes through two dirty windows in the back of the van. Its dream-like effect creating my reality. Revealing like ghosts my unexpected company.

The cigarette smoke, not lucky enough to have escaped, was trapped. It lazily floated in the air adding to the already surrealness of it all. Backpacks and wood crates littered the floor of the interior. I found my spot and settled in for the ride. From the shadows, an apparition spoke. "I'm Tino. How is my friend Tony doin?" Johnny B said Senior was sending a good friend of his and to maybe keep an eye on 'em."

His voice was croaky from smoking too much weed, and he kept licking his lips. Despite my current situation, I couldn't help smiling to myself. Then another voice, deeper and more committed to the moment. "My name is Benny... they call me Cha-Cha cause I love to dance and love the ladies. He leaned forward into my dream scene and reached out to shake my hand. His right hand moved in jagged patterns as we bounced along. "Welcome, my brother. Good to have you with us, cause we are all brothers now."

"I'm Stevie, nice to meet you guys."

The ghosts escaped back into the shadows of the van where the light wouldn't go, satisfied at their introductions. I sat there in the fading light of a NYC late afternoon, smoking a cigarette. We all had run out of anything to say. The Zombies were singing on the radio, *"It is the time of the season for lov...ing."*

SLIPPING INTO DARKNESS
NOVEMBER, 1974

Those that worked during the war overseas and not in uniform were a distinct stock of humans. Ex-military or ex-CIA. Most with the experience necessary to perform covert operations, something we never took part in. More importantly, training and schooling us in eight weeks in all that we needed to know to survive. It was grueling, enlightening . . . life changing. These (mostly) men were drawn in by a mix of motives and circumstances. Warped idealism, high salaries, and a taste for blood, not their own, if you get my meaning. Most not feeling at home, at home. Then there were guys like me, Cha-Cha, and Tino, mixed in for the heavy lifting mostly, here for "our own reasons."

Regardless, reason or excuse, here we all were up to our necks in a shit-show of unprecedented proportions. Toward the end of the war, there were dozens of private contracting companies, bringing opium and weed (never heroin) in and out of the country, making huge sums of cash for these "private contractor companies." (Although I couldn't and would never swear to what I did. All the crates were unmarked.) At the same time, the North Vietnamese spent their time smuggling in weapons from both China and Russia to support their war effort and their troops, not get them addicted. By the time we got there, for a lot of people on both sides and no side at all, heroin was their choice of poison. Weed was second nature like a pack of Winstons, the preferred brand. I had sworn a blood oath kissing Senior on each cheek promising to stay far away from heroin. As he put it, "Turn your back on it and forget it exists." So it was, none of us ever got near "H" in any way, shape, or form. Senior wasn't who he was because he didn't know about everything. He knew everything, everyone he knew involved with it had died. Either by it or from it.

So, we stayed far away. We talked it over, the three of us, Me, Cha Cha, and Tino, as we always did, unanimously deciding there was enough needless addiction, death, and blood surrounding us already. The young men getting blown up and maimed for absolutely nothing, in the end, deserved better. They became like family, they didn't need to do that. God bless them, to this day I thank them all.

Long Khanh – January, 1975 – We had been in Cambodia for the past two months, receiving and sending "supplies" and loading them onto choppers, mixed in with munitions and medical supplies delivered into South Vietnam by Chinooks to the ARVN (Army of the Republic of Vietnam). We watched the Northern Highlands' rapid fall to the North's well-armed brutal advance against the valiant but scattered retreat of the South Vietnamese. Finally, it was our turn to move farther south into Vietnam, toward Saigon, with the supplies. We boarded the Chinook.

Long Khanh (pronounced Long Khan) had seen its share of fighting back in 1970 but was safe enough for now. It was where we would set up base. It was twenty-three kilometers northwest of a place called Xuan Loc (pronounced swan luck), which was the gateway to Saigon another one-hundred-and-six kilometers south. The North had started its Spring Offensive. This was to be the decisive and final push south toward capturing Saigon on April 30th, only seven weeks later. We were stationed with a small unit of Marines who had our backs and flew us in and out of Long Khanh and Xuan Loc. Not carrying "supplies" any longer but delivering medical supplies and munitions, then helping transport out the wounded and the dead.

The battle for Xuan Loc could be the last great battle of the war. The AVRN had dug in and were told to hold Xuan Loc at all costs. The battle raged for twelve days. From dawn on April 9th through April 21st, the city took eight thousand rounds of heavy artillery fire. Within days, we bore witness to the bloody and hard truth of just how faithless and determined the PAVN (People's Army Of Vietnam) was. We performed as asked, as the number of dead and wounded piled up all around us. As the fighting and shelling deepened, we transported medical supplies, food, and weapons, never once engaging the enemy unless all other options had been exhausted. It was not in our contract. Nevertheless, we dodged bullets and rocket fire and did the best we could to support the Marines and our South Vietnamese allies any way we could. We decided, at that point, that we were there to do as we were asked without question and to offer our extreme service. Doing what was needed anyway we could.

TINO TAKES A DIVE AND CHA-CHA'S LAST DANCE
XUAN LOC – JANUARY 1975

The Chinook, armed with only one 7.62 mm M60 machine gun, off the left side door, hovered thirty feet off the ground over the drop zone in the pitch black pouring fucking rain, exchanging ground fire from what seemed like everywhere. The sound, shattering, disabling. I was certain, without question, I was going to die. That we were all going to die.

The last time I saw Tino alive, the guy that was supposed to watch over me for Senior, he was rocking back and forth with his hands over his ears, eyes darting around wildly, tears streaming from his eyes, seemingly popping out of their sockets. We were all petrified with the idea of getting shot and dying. Getting captured or losing a limb. I had never experienced this type of violence.

What had Senior done? Lower, lower, I jumped at fifteen feet instead of waiting for us to drop closer, praying for a safe landing with sixty pounds of kit on my back. My first jump looked a lot closer than it actually was. I'm thinking a hard landing was better than getting hit with a bullet. What the fuck did I know?

For a minute, time and space had come to cessation, seconds later materializing once again as I plowed into the rain-soaked ground landing on my back. Wet, sore, and dazed, I laid there for what seemed like forever but was, again, only seconds.

"Holy shit, you're a crazy-man. If you break something out here, you are in fucked city, amigo, you copy? I do not understand what the fuck you were trying to do, but do not ever do that shit again. Looks like you bit your lip on the way down. Wipe that blood off," all the while patting me down looking for more blood and broken bones. He was totally present, aware of each movement around us. "You can get both of us killed trying to save your dumb ass. Do you fuckin' copy?" We rose to a hunched-back posture and I see he is a Marine.

"Can you walk?"

"Yes, I'm fine." We stood fully, in unison, as one being, me following his directions to the letter. "Come on, let's go. Step exactly into my footprints, this field is loaded with mines." The guy helped me up off the ground the same way Tony had done a lifetime ago lifting off the street, ten thousand miles and thousands of years away.

Finally, he relaxed. "Come on. I got your back, brother."

I remember mumbling back between my, once again, historically bloody lips. "Who the fuck are you?"

"My name is Leon. Now let's split before we both get shot."

I never saw him again. God bless you, Leon, wherever you are.

I found out that night that Tino had died. He had broken his neck falling out of the doorway of the bouncing craft, waiting to jump off. The chopper swayed like a pendulum, back and forth, dodging incoming fire. Cha-Cha said that one second Tino was there, then he was gone. The same fifteen feet in the air that I had conquered, had killed him. That is how it was over there. Kind of, now you see it, now you don't.

I watched as they unloaded his body off the chopper. I remember seeing his head sitting on his shoulders at an impossible angle as they carried him past us on a stretcher as if held on only by sinew and flesh, his head swaying back and forth. It felt as though in death he was in denial of his own passing. Tino, whose last name I never knew, who promised to watch over me, whose face was easy to look at, was now just the revolting, repellent remains of another asinine, and nonsensical, death. They lowered, then rested the stretcher on the ground and respectfully lifted Tino off the stretcher and into the maw of another hungry body bag, ready to swallow his remains whole. Blood slid down his face, running from his ears then off the side of his mouth in big drops, mixing with the blood of other warriors that had been carried, dead or alive, on the same, tired stretcher before him.

Tino was a Jersey boy, denied admittance into the regular Army for whatever reasons we never got around to hearing about, now forever unknown. A good friend, who left us in an unexpected and violent manner, in a place none of us belonged.

Days and responsibility morphed into weeks of supply and survival. We carried on with tears in our eyes. Fear tried its best to consume me, but I wouldn't let it, not yet.

ARVN and civilian casualties continued to climb, leaving us to begin wondering if we were making any difference at all. Tino, Cha-Cha, and I had just started sharing our stories of home, women, sports, and family and what we wanted to do when we got back Stateside. We got close. What a fuckin' mistake. Apparitions as they appeared in the back of the van the day we met; ghosts they became to me when they died. Haunting me at times to this day. So sorry, Tino.

It was about two months later, Cha-Cha got blown up stepping on a toe popper outside the wire one night taking a dump. Dumbass. The North Vietnamese called them "dap loi" or "min muoi" (mosquito mines). They were made from empty 50-caliber machine gun shells filled with gunpowder and scraps of metal. He got blown to fucking pieces. Dry mouth and heaving, we scooped together whatever we could find of him, placing his left arm, a leg, and other body parts in a body bag. Then, as fast as humanly possible, reverently taking his remains with us before the shit rained down, our position being exposed by the explosion. We all go home. No one gets left behind. No more dancing for Cha-Cha. Even if he had lived, we had only found his right leg anyway.

February, 1975 – Three months later we boarded an Army transport leaving Tan Son Nhut Air Base in South Vietnam carrying dozens of the battered and other fortunate. A puzzle of Vietnamese women and children, guys like us, and regular Army. First to Frankfurt, Germany, then on a commercial flight back home. Saigon, along with Tan Son, fell to the north two months later, April 30, 1975.

As the transport lifted off the ground, we all knew we had beat the odds and made it out alive.

In the real world, you all thought you were being informed of what was going on as you watched the conflict on the evening news in living color. You had no fucking idea what it was like. The Vietnam war was a cluster fuck, beginning to end. A sick game with no winners, only a loss column. Millions died needlessly on both sides, some of whom still carry scars of the conflict with them today. Both internal and external. War . . . what a fuckin' waste.

MEMBERS ONLY
KENNEDY AIRPORT – FEBRUARY, 1975

The Boeing 727 sliced its way through brown, syrupy smog that seemed to thicken as the sun rose. Its presence momentarily blocked. The shifting light through the cabin of the plane retrieved me from sleep. I lifted up the shade that covered my window, which left me staring at golden brick buildings with thousands of windows, awakening, bright looking like hot, golden honey, as if each room behind them was on fire. I sat back, closing my eyes to the spectacle, head against the backrest, arms crossed against my chest, seat belt fastened. Relieved. Unimpressed.

I had called the club collect from the airport in Frankfurt. Senior answered the phone, accepting the charges. He genuinely sounded both thrilled and relieved to hear my voice. I remember the deep sense of relief I felt when he said, "Welcome home, kid." I told him where and when Jerry and Tony needed to meet me. In retrospect, it's funny how I assumed they were there, back at the club safe and sound. I wondered if they ever expected to see me again.

As I walked through the gates back onto American soil, there were no marching bands or signs saying welcome home. No family or family dog to hug and embrace. There was no hot housewife holding a baby. Just two Lower East Side dudes in deep burgundy, matching *Members Only* jackets and bright white Tee-shirts. One fat and one skinny, one wearing jeans and sneakers, the other slacks and black shoes. Cigarettes balanced in the corner of their mouths, smiling, coughing from the smoke, laughing. Genuinely happy to see me. I took a deep breath. It felt good to be back. It was good to see them. Tony looked thinner and tired. Jerry was still fat, but tan from his extended hiatus somewhere south of the border.

The big man came bounding over, "Holy shit, kid, welcome back. We missed you. Things weren't the same without you." I hugged them both simultaneously, and Tony whispered into my ear, "I can only imagine." Stepping back, then standing there like Fonzie on *Happy Days*, he was relieved that I was back in one fucking piece. I remember seeing it in his eyes. We had that bond from day one. He stepped forward, leaned in, and whispered a second time, "Hey, Stevie, I missed you, you dumb fuck." We walked out of the international terminal at JFK Airport into the sunlight, arm in arm, three grown men, tough guys, comrades, brothers, and at that moment, once again untouchable. Three little assholes.

We drove back in Jerry's Buick, taking the Grand Central Parkway west to the BQE, then over the Williamsburg Bridge, smoking a joint. We landed on Delancey Street. As we came off the bridge, Junior tossed me twenty-five thousand dollars in a brand-new, black backpack. I inspected the bag of neatly stacked fifties and hundreds.

"There ya go, kid. Senior saved and held the money himself for you."

I sat in the back of the Buick, stoned, and cried my eyes out knowing it was okay to let go in front of these men.

The dead child molester with his balls missing, which had forced our collective departure, had blown over and was dead and buried, so to speak. Senior had done what he promised. I was good to go. The street was quiet.

A CAGE FULL OF GHOSTS
JULY, 1975

It had been five months since my return. Being home felt safe enough but mostly overwhelming. Too much concrete, too many windows, and way too many fuckin' people. Each life that had been left behind ten thousand miles away had carved a hole in my brain. The pain of each death chipped away at me. I lay awake at night asking myself, *Why them and not me?* And always, from the grave, Tino and Cha-Cha's ceaseless reply, *Why us, brother? Why us and not you?*

Cha-Cha's death was a never-ending graphic slow-motion movie in my head. Collecting what was left of him, our ears still ringing from the explosion. His body parts scattered twenty yards in every God-damn direction. Blood dripped off the leaves and branches where pieces and parts of him had landed. What was left of him humped together in a mess of entrails, bone, and flesh.

When Tino broke his neck falling fifteen feet to his death, it was so sudden and unexpected that none of us had time to react properly to his death. I lived with his surprise and his fear every night and whenever I was alone. And I was never alone. All that I had seen was like a fresh salted wound. Especially at night in the dark. Tino's broken body filled my vision every time I closed my eyes. There was no rest to be found here. My cousin's place had become a cage full of ghosts. It was time to go.

One morning after a torturous night of visitations, I walked to Senior's club and asked to use the phone to call my father at his place of work. After all I had witnessed and participated in both here and over there, my mother still filled my mind with raw, childlike fear. Monsters always will.

I dialed my dad's shop's phone number from a rotary payphone hanging on the wall in the back of the club that never needed any coins or ever ran out of minutes. After three rings, my dad's, craggy, smoker's voice, said cheerfully, "Good morning, Villa TV!"

My father's voice, after so long.

The good guy in me, the man I was soon to become, was not yet understanding that love was the ultimate power. That love's sword and shield are forged in the light love produced. Anything can be said without judgment, as long as it's said with and in the name of love. So simple, right? Back in those days, the dark overlord of shit ruled all my emotions. Stealth and cunning, not letting me unburden what had become an emotional appendage, infected and needing to be cut off.

Where I had been, the people I had killed. Why I had gone in the first place. Like the cold hands of a corpse rising out of the ground and pulling me under, filling my mouth with dead dirt, all I managed to express, as matter-of-factly as I could, was something like, "Hey Dad, been a while."

"So glad you called, son, I've . . . the family has missed you. Good to have you back. Will we be seeing you soon, Stevie?" I heard his love for me, his expectation. His uneasiness in possibly not seeing me after all this time. I needed my father in my life desperately, especially knowing he felt my need and pain as it peppered the empty space between us.

"I really missed you too, Dad. I'm fine. Give my love to everyone. We will see each other soon, I promise." I hung up halfway through his goodbye. Ashamed, wiping tears from my face, I walked to Dominic's for my usual two slices and a Coke. I hardly touched it.

Seven years after crash landing, then living in this odd and beautiful concrete wilderness called the Lower East Side, amongst its creatures, surviving, I was once again taking flight. Not from its rooftops, not from its people, places, or its things. I was running from my undeniable attraction to its sheltered, and easily adaptable, existence.

That next morning I stuffed all my socks and underwear, my toothbrush, and one extra pair of jeans into a backpack and walked away, leaving my bat Excalibur in the closet with its posse of demons and clowns, locked in its darkness. They banged on the door crying to be taken. Crying for their freedom. The bat trying to persuade me, *You're not safe out there in the world without me, Stevie. Who will protect you? Stevie, Stevie, Stevie.*

Fading, *Don't... leeavee... meee...*

I traversed down from the fourth floor for what I knew would be the last time, carrying a small gym bag with the money, backpack with my clothing and toothbrush, and three thousand in fifties in my front left pocket. I slowed instinctively as I passed Mrs. Facetti's apartment, now all cleaned up and occupied by a young Irish family. I opened the front door to the building and out onto its cracked and dirty steps. In the light of this new day, it's thrones nothing more than a nasty place to park your lazy ass. No place for a real king to hold court. Not anymore anyway.

As usual, the streets were humming, full of daytime hustle, conspiracy, and trade. I walked over to Senior's club, making my way through the crowds and the hellos. When I got there, he was sitting at the big table putting numbers and notes in a big ledger, which he closed when he saw me walk in. He was surprised to see me. I handed him all my earnings – less three thousand dollars. I knew my money was safer with Senior than any bank. We sat at the big table, and he listened to my parting remarks. He took the money and said good-bye, knowing things would never be the same again between us. No hugs or best wishes, no see you soon, keep in touch.

"Take care, Stevie, I'm deeply sorry things turned out the way they did. I had no idea at all as to what I was sending you into. If I would have known I, I . . ."

He had run out of words.

I filled in the blanks for him. "Please, say good-bye to Tony." If Tony would have been there, I never would have left; he was like a brother to me. If he'd asked me to say a little longer, I would have. "I will call from time to time." We hugged, leaving our tears on each other's shoulders. I turned and left the club. Fat Jerry opened the door for me with a pat on the back. I knew he watched me walk away. I took the subway to Port Authority and boarded a Greyhound bus to Vermont, for no other reason except that it was the first place that came to mind. When I got to Stowe, I turned left, stuck out my thumb, and headed west, hitching the rest of the way across the country. I felt the need for a big sky and vast stretches of land. To walk again unarmed and unafraid.

SAINT DERRICK
NOVEMBER, 1975

I had made it to the state of Washington, deciding it was time to cross the border into Canada. I had settled on Vancouver as my first stop. Late one night after not sleeping for days, I managed to catch a ride at a rest stop with a trucker hauling supplies north, figuring the driver would know most of the border crossings. As the truck shifted its gears onto the highway, I asked the driver which crossing would be the best without really being noticed. He smiled knowingly, asked me my name and where my accent was from, and extended his hand, embracing mine. His name was Derrick. He looked and spoke like the Jesus I would have imagined. Maybe it was lack of sleep or the halo the cabin light of the truck cast around him.

There is no illusion, only real magic, barreling safely down a deserted mountain highway at 65 miles an hour at 2:00 a.m. with Jesus at the wheel.

Listening to country music with the heater pumping out warm air and the faint smell of the diesel engine. The lights of the dashboard emitting a low yellowish glow. The hum of the tires and the way my ass fit perfectly into the bucket seat. Derrick shared his mug of hard tasting black coffee, tuna sandwiches on white bread, and homemade chocolate cupcakes his wife had baked. Enjoyed in accompanied silence of our digestion and Johnny Cash.

I told Derrick about the Lower East Side of Manhattan but not how I had ended up there. I told him about Jimmy Fingers, Tony, and Mr. Lee. About Dominic's Pizzeria and the deaths of my cousin Bobby, Mrs. Facetti, and my friend Larry. I told him that my childhood had not been an easy one and that I had left at an early age to, as I saw it, save my own life. Ending with, "I was overseas for a while, got back five months ago, needed to see some open space, so I hit the road."

Softly unannounced, after a time, Derrick spoke. He had a wife and two little girls, a mortgage on his house back in Montana, and monthly payments on his truck. Derrick had hauled produce and building supplies up into Canada for the past thirteen years. He had road-weary hands and the lines of untold miles on his face. The cabin of the truck was his home, office, and bedroom. There was a huge white plastic cross glued to the dashboard. Pictures of his wife, little girls, and his truck were stuck into the vents and visors. The radio played an unnamed country song, lamenting lost love. The constant chatter of the CB radio.

Then I told him everything, coming clean to a stranger. I gave it all up and let it all out. It was cathartic and confessional. Maybe it was the tuna sandwiches and coffee, maybe it was the truck's heater or the plush leather seats that cradled me. There was no judgment in his questions, only acceptance in his posture. His eyes never left mine. He heard everything I didn't say. We were strangers in the cabin of a truck in the middle of the night when the journey first started hours ago. Now there was only fellowship and trust. Knowing I'd never see this person again had been my motive at first to unburden myself. But it had turned into a moment that would never be forgotten, for my entire life. When I was done, we drove in silence as he took it all in. When he finally spoke again, he was fascinated by the stories, seeing New York City as this magical concrete jungle of lunatics and lawlessness. He asked me what it was like to live in a place like that. I told him it was hard to describe. Telling him to look me up if he ever got there and I'd show him around, knowing that that would never happen. We looked at each other differently for the rest of the way, with a kind of mutual respect and understanding of who each of us was. He pulled out his map and explained where I would be when he dropped me off, suggesting the Osoyoos crossing.

"Listen, kid, I'm going to drop you off in Oroville. Just head north and follow the signs through town to the border. The crossing is a metal bridge over a small gully with two border guards on the U.S side. For ten dollars each and a hot cup of coffee, they're your best friends for three minutes. Here's twenty bucks, you look like you can use it."

He pointed on the map, covering the exact location with the width of his index finger, "It is in the middle of nowhere. Been there for years. A lot of people have been crossing back and forth since the war. Road is full of young people. Good luck, son. God bless you."

"Maybe he will, sir. Thank you for your friendship."

With a hiss and a sigh, both driver and truck pulled to a stop at the town limits of Oroville. I jumped down onto the black top and thanked him. We said good-bye without ever exchanging a handshake. We had passed that minor formality, sharing the stories of our lives and black coffee sixty miles back.

PRAISE THE LORD AND PASS THE BISCUITS
NOVEMBER 1975

I was now four miles from the Canadian border. I had traveled about as far west and as far north in my homeland as I could. Walking toward town, I passed a white, sun-stained, wood sign mounted on two wood posts with clear but faded green block lettering:

Welcome to Oroville

Population 1555

Jesus Saves

No Hippies

Underneath on a separate plank of wood was listed several rotary clubs and churches with their accompanying symbols, along with the name of the current mayor. Oroville was no more than a large, paved intersection in 1975. It had a luncheonette, two small bars, a movie house (which back in the day was a burlesque theater), two churches, one Episcopalian, one Catholic, a general/feed store and post office/barber shop. There was an auto-repair shop and gas station farther down the road on the other side of the railroad tracks, and small train station that housed a Western Union. I slowed my pace and took it all in. The surrounding hills and valleys were covered in apple orchards, now all bare. Dairy farms and small groups of grazing cattle dotted the fall landscape. The muffled distant clap of dishes in someone's kitchen, sounds of kids playing somewhere blocks away. The everyday sounds of another every day in a small town.

Autumn's golden grace and beauty filled the air. I was attracted by what I would now define writing it all down as its Americanism and intimacy. My feet, unguided, carrying my body forward as a passenger not of my own free will. Heading north, following the signs to the Osoyoos crossing, my feet took a right onto Main Street toward the small bridge to Canada. The growing sounds of gospel music and fellowship, accompanied by the smell of roasting meat, altered my intention and direction instantly. Following the sound of laughter and song, and the unmistakable smell of BBQ, my feet made another right onto Central Avenue, crossing to the lake side of the street. There stood the Trinity Episcopal Church, a red brick, nondescript cliché. It stood on the corner surrounded by trees, small shrubs, and bushes. There were benches out front for the town's faithful and small checker tables in the shade of the building's cross on the south side. As I passed by the church celebration, a man's voice called out to me. I stopped, turned, and saw Pastor Mike for the first time. A small, round, young man with tasseled brown hair, big teeth, and ice blue eyes waving hello, as if to an old friend he hadn't seen in a while. Behind him in the church yard were dozens of people sitting together in small rows of picnic benches, bundled in winter coats, warmed by the grace of their God, singing, eating and laughing in the forty-plus degree weather. In fellowship, they carried on.

"Welcome to Oroville, young man. Do you know God? Because he knows you and he loves you."

"Yes, I've heard of him, sir, thanks . . ." It was a sarcastic, unfair reply. Exposing my weariness. I continued, "I don't think he would want much to do with me right now, sir."

"God loves you no matter what you have done or think you have done. There is a place at God's table in heaven and on this earth for us all." He went on, "Have you been baptized, son?"

Was he blind or just fuckin' kidding? I politely replied, "No, sir, I haven't."

SWIMMING WITH GOD: NOVEMBER'S END, 1975

The Okanogan River in November, as best can be described, was a humanly intolerable, freezing mass of rapidly moving liquid. Mike the priest gently as the hand of God held my head in the palm of his right hand, pressing his left hand on my chest over my heart, drawing me back into the water; I let go. Letting the frigid, rushing water run over me. Separating me from the world, opening me to my core, cleansing a part of me. Making me aware of its presence in no uncertain terms. Revealing not so much the spirit of God but the power that it held if accepted.

At twenty-one years old, it would be decades until I embraced the light and love that was given to me on that day. I would not allow entry of these deep blessings. But as blessings go, they stuck around and let themselves in without asking for permission at the right times and in the right places . . . repeatedly.

I was wrapped in a warm wool blanket and given clean warm clothes that almost fit. Drinking hot black coffee, stuffing my mouth, and watching my knapsack being packed with enough containers of roast chicken and biscuits, sweet fall apples, and butter cookies. Enough for the next week. I remember sleeping on a cot in the back of the church later that evening and waking in the middle of the night to leave. The finality of good-bye scared me. How many people in my life so far had I said good-byes to and never seen alive again. The memory of Mrs. Facetti stung the corners of my eyes.

Pastor Mike was lying in wait for what he had seen so many times before with young men like me. Passing through town on their way to the footbridge to Canada. Lost, drifting, in search of what he never asked to know, and no one ever told him.

"Here," he said, handing me a warm pair of his own gloves. A hug, a nod of the head, and I was gone. Thank you, Pastor Mike. Your tender heart and kindness in our brief time together resurrected the spirit within me. Look at me, a baptized Jewish kid, now best friends with Jesus. Praise the Lord and pass the biscuits.

THE STORY OF CHRISTMAS, LAONI, ANGEL

CANADA - DECEMBER, 1975

I remember distinctly almost sauntering across that narrow, slightly swaying metal pedestrian bridge into Canada like I was king of the world. I remember thinking, look at me, look at me.

I crossed the border without incident. The guards knew the drill. They thanked me for the coffee and the butter cookies, stuffed the money in their pockets, wishing me their insincere best. Thankful for the twenty-dollars Derrick had handed me to grease their wheels, and the butter cookies from Pastor Mike and his congregation.

Walking at an accelerated pace in the pitch black, reading the map Derrick had given me with a flashlight, I followed it to the closest paved road and stuck out my thumb. Catching rides due west to Vancouver, two-hundred and forty miles away. Passing through towns and cities with names like Copper Mountain, Sunshine Valley, Flood, and Bridal Falls. First along Route 3, then finally onto the Trans Canadian Highway (Route 1) outside of Hope, where both highways intersected.

Five rides, too much dishonest conversation with strangers, and a lot of walking, I was twenty miles away from my destination.

Sunrise, day two. Vancouver's skyline slowly lifted the morning fog above its knees, exposing its skeletal frame of glass and brick. Hours later I crossed her city limits. Slowing my pace, easing myself into the city's pool of people. I walked around for what seemed like hours. Letting the streets absorb me. Like fresh water running through the gills of a goldfish in a new tank of water, its multitudes of humanity filtered through me, thrilling me in my new surroundings.

After roaming around for what seemed like hours, my eyes settled on a cluster of barren brown trees in a public park two blocks away. It was cold outside, but I needed to sit down. I had been walking all day, my feet hurt. I didn't want to break my last ten dollar bill sitting in a pub or diner until my money ran out just to warm up. I was hoping to find a youth hostel or three dollar a night flophouse to crash in overnight. A hot soapy shower and sleeping in a warm bed seemed particularly important. No matter which one of these two options made themselves available to me, either one would be a blessing. Another chilly night outside was becoming harder and harder.

Queen Elizabeth Park. I saw them for the first time, standing at the front of the closed, black iron gates at the park's entrance with the park's name on it. They seemed to be asking for change and something to eat. They both looked cold and tired. As I walked closer, I heard them wishing everyone a Merry Christmas, which was just under three weeks away. People hurried by glancing at them for a guilty nano-second. Hands filled with mostly gifts or some such thing and some Christmas trees. Both of them were wrapped in sweaters, hats, gloves or mittens, and oversized coats. I knew right away that they were mother and daughter. The little girl was pushed up against her mom, with one hand in the pocket of her mother's coat and the other hand in the pocket of her own coat. I remember that like a photo to this day . . . striking me as my initial impression of them. Trust. She seemed to be about seven years old and was wearing a too big Santa hat that almost covered her chestnut brown curls.

As I got closer, I noticed a well-used coffee can with some money inside of it sitting on the ground between them. There were no food containers or bags to be seen. There was no way for me to tell how long they had been standing in that spot or how far they had traveled to get here. This is how my mind thought back then. Observe, assess, plan, execute. Still works.

I saw the little girl pointing at me, then tugging on her mother's coat. Most likely wanting to know who that guy was in an army jacket staring at them as he walked into the corner store directly across the street. I broke the ten and bought three large hot chocolates with extra whipped cream for the little girl. I left the store with eight dollars and fifty cents. I walked over, said hello, and handed the first container to the mom, then asked if I could give her little girl the second container. With her mother's approval, I slowly bent down and placed the large hot container into the girl's grateful little hands, meeting her face-to-face with a smile. Watching her looking at the whipped cream with gleeful intention, then smiling back.

As I straightened up, her mother had visibly softened from the steaming sweet reprieve cupped in her hands. She had pulled off her hat, revealing the same shoulder length, chestnut brown curls that had been hidden underneath her daughter's hat. She had piercing blue eyes. Her gaze was deep and true. I couldn't look away. In a second that felt like a lifetime, she seemed to somehow know my sum total. Pain will always sense pain. Time slowed to a crawl, although my heart denied itself of that reality, beating on my chest to be let free. Then she said, "Thanks, mister. That's real-nice of you, it tastes wonderful."

Still transfixed, "Your little girl's smile is enough for me, you're welcome."

Taken aback, she looked away. Releasing us both from our locked gaze. Looking down, focusing her eyes and attention toward her daughter. "My name's Angel; this is my daughter, Laoni. Thank you for the hot chocolate. That's truly kind of you, mister, really."

"My name is Steve," fumbling, "are you guys hungry? I have a backpack full of chicken, biscuits, and some apples." Without waiting for debate, I unzipped my knapsack and handed out the food. A hard life is an easy tell. We moved over to the row of benches outside the locked gates and sat down.

Fear shows its defiance in two ways. A head-on, eye-to-eye stare, or a slight casting down of the eyes with an almost invisible flinch. I knew them both very well. I had seen them in the eyes of many men.

Angel looked at the food laid out on the bench then locked into me again. Her telepathic look said to me what I already knew, *I know you get that I'm doing the best I can with what I have for my little girl.* She was strong, providing for the little one in her life. Immediately, it deepened my unannounced attraction.

Laoni looked at me, tugging on my jacket, leaving chicken-finger fingerprints on its sleeve. Displaying a large chocolate and whip cream mustache, wrapped around her smile. "Do you live around here, Mr. Steve?"

I bent down, her breath was warm and smelled like chocolate and dough from the biscuits, which she was now dipping in her cooling hot chocolate. Pieces of chicken were stuck between her teeth. She possessed an unmistakable aura of hope and innocence that surrounded her. You could feel it, and it was contagious. In my seven decades on this planet, I haven't felt that from any other child or adult again. Her love made me feel complete. Even in my own loneliness. I replied, "No sweetheart, I'm just passing through."

"Don't you have a place to stay?" she asked.

"No, not yet."

Then as out of the ordinary as this day was turning into, a huge, unexpected turn. "Mom, can Mr. Steve stay with us?"

Her mother looked at her, then to me, then to her daughter once again with a slight smirk. "Sure, why not. As long as he promises to behave."

In less than thirty minutes, things shifted, just by showing kindness to strangers as it had been shown to me. Whatever Pastor Mike had seemed to be contagious. Angels and hot chocolate. Who knew?

Mother and daughter shared a one-bedroom walk-up on the second floor of a stand-alone house on Walden Street. Walking distance from the park where I had first seen them.

The first thing I noticed was Laoni's artwork. Colorful visions of fields and flowers, sunshine, and dancing animals with happy faces. Like wallpaper, these crayoned creations festooned the refrigerator, kitchen cabinets, doors to each room, and all of the living room walls. Each drawing had two figures. One big, one small.

Child's eye detail held these images in high regard. Showing the symbiotic nature, love and partnership Laoni had created equally with her mother. Their intense love and connection upon walking into this world of colorful consciousness was intense.

A pair of clean, second-hand curtains was carefully hung above the one small living room window with tacks and duct tape. A huge 1950s, seen-better-day-style sofa piled with neatly stacked blankets and sleeping pillows at each end, took up most of the far wall. There was a tiny black-and-white television on a kitchen table, its rabbit ears antenna covered in little blue, sparkly ribbons. A folding card table with four chairs, covered in a plastic Christmas tablecloth, was tucked into the corner under another window that faced the street next to an immaculately clean kitchen. A four-foot silver Christmas tree sat at the side of the sofa perched on a cardboard box also covered in Christmas cheer. Its tiny lights illuminating the scant offerings of gifts from mother to daughter.

The bathroom was halfway down a short hallway. To the right was Laoni's room. Angel slept on the sofa every night so her daughter could feel special having her own room. She had done the best she could to make the place a home for her little girl. They had everything they needed. They had each other.

Again, a gentle, insistent tugging on the sleeve of my army jacket.

"Mr. Steven, Mr. Steven!" The excitement and love poured from this little creature and made my heart skip a beat. I knelt down in front of her.

"Yes, little one, what can I do for you?"

"I just asked mama. She said you can share the sofa and there are clean towels and soap if you wanna take a shower. Mama said to leave your clothes on the floor in the hallway because they smell really bad."

She then proceeded to take me by the hand, wrapping her whole right hand around my index finger, and led me down the hallway to the bathroom, as if leading a horse to its stable. Pointing with her finger where I should leave my dirty clothes, I was warned with a smile that I had better include my "nasty underwear." Our first few nights sharing the sofa we slept toe to toe at opposite end. We developed harmony. Right down to the bedtime stories we both read to Laoni every night before her good-night prayers.

The simple pleasure of holding a woman on a sofa under a pile of soft blankets as the temperature dropped to single digits outside and the snow came down was intoxicating. It had been a very long time. Katie's face came to me fleetingly.

The last time I had been with Katie was when I was fifteen-years-old. That had been five, intensely long years ago. Angel and I listened to *Ladies of The Canyon* on a small single speaker record player over and over while the Christmas tree blinked on and off, seemingly in time to the sound of each note. Simple pleasures of safety and peace with one another. Safety, something both of us had not been comforted by in a long time.

Then on Christmas Eve after we had put Laoni to bed, finally inviting me in, she whispered in my ear that she wanted me and that she loved me. Angel's body was sweet and warm. She was musky, female, soft, and soft spoken. With great need and intention, I responded. I told her I loved her and Laoni. We folded into each other's bodies making love all night in between short naps and fits of laughter. Waking up Christmas morning, naked and wrapped around each other under a pile of blankets, smelling of our sex. Making love one last time in the light of Christmas morning, bad breath and all. I remember Laoni running out of her room jumping on top of us screaming, "It's Christmas, it's Christmas, get up, get up

. . . Santa left me gifts." She had rainbows and candy canes in her eyes that morning. The glee of that moment danced all around her. Turning us all into children on Christmas. She laughed at us sleeping together, asked what we were doing, and requested breakfast. It all seemed quite natural. Pancakes, anyone?

The winter of 1976 and the next three years were a joyful time for all three of us. Laoni was off to school in the morning; Angel and I off to work if we were lucky enough. We lived off Angel's government assistance and whatever we could make doing odd jobs, both making sure Laoni was taken care of. I worked as a handyman and dishwasher around town, being careful and trying to remain as low key as possible, knowing I was there in Canada as an illegal worker no matter how comfortable I became. I knew one thing from my days on the streets of the Lower East Side working for Senior. Lay low, don't say shit, and carry a big stick. Of course, I followed his orders to the letter. For the most part I avoided idle talk at work and when invited out for a beer or two with the guys.

Angel worked part time three days a week at a local pet store taking care of a small menagerie of small birds and animals. It paid and was within walking distance of the house. Laoni loved stopping by on her way home from school to see her mom and look at all the small animals and fish tanks full of tropical fish.

As time went by, I released bits of my history. Telling just enough, answering her questions as best as I could, without going into too much detail as to how I ended up here in the first place. She kept most of her past to herself. Telling me about her childhood, growing up, her wild years, and where they were now, but never how they got here.

She never spoke of Laoni's father, even when I tried to bring it up. Where he was or what happened to him. I asked her once, and she told me it was a discussion for another time as she drew me in under the blankets, putting her hands on me, making me forget what my question was. I didn't press her; I loved her at that moment; we were together. We celebrated our birthdays and cooked

Thanksgiving dinners. We took care of each other. Our lives were low key and under the radar just the way I liked it. I hadn't felt so connected to and surrounded by real love since my childhood with my grandparents. Laoni was now ten years old and had taken to calling me Papa Steve. We talked about making plans, moving to a bigger place with a backyard for Laoni to run around in. Maybe even a puppy. I thought of applying for citizenship.

BILLY COMES HOME
SPRING, 1979

For weeks Angel had been acting strange and noticeably distracted when we were together under the blankets. "Billy, Laoni's father, is getting out of prison in two weeks. He was locked up for six years, serving a ten-year sentence. He just made parole on good behavior."

"Why didn't you tell me this three years ago when you had the chance? Why was he away, for what?"

"Aggravated assault, armed robbery, and possession of a weapon."

"Holy crap, Angel."

"I didn't think it mattered. Ten years is a long time. I expected Laoni and I to be long gone by the time he got out. I've had no contact at all until the phone call the other day from the prison telling me he will be released and will be coming back to live with us. The courts and the system have nothing to keep him away from us. Since he never harmed me and has never seen his daughter, there is nothing they can do. If anything, they believe this environment is good for him to make a clean start, with a family and all. I haven't figured out a way to tell Laoni yet. She has no idea."

"Fuck this shit... I love you and Laoni."

"I love *you*, my dear man. My daughter loves you. I thought we could be a family. I was lost in your kindness and attention, my darling. I am sorry, Steven."

"We can leave before he gets out, Angel. You have no ties to this place or to him. Laoni can go to school anywhere. She has no idea he even exists."

"I can't do that, baby. Some part of me still cares about him. If he made a mistake and has seen the wrong in what he did and wants to see his daughter, what can I do except to give him a chance?"

I couldn't argue. She had her reasons. Angel was not going to change her mind. I had known her long enough to know that.

"Did he ever harm or threaten you?"

"No, my love, never. Promise."

In a trance induced by surprise and now, founded in sorrow, "Okay then, I'll leave in the morning."

We both could feel the present swirling around us as realization sank in, infecting all we had built together the past three years. In its best moments, life isn't ready for what you ask of it, and in return, you never get what you expect.

Appropriately, it was cold, grey, and very early in the morning when we said our goodbyes. We had decided for now to tell Laoni that I was going away for work and would be back as soon as I could. It was up to her mom to explain the rest. I didn't envy either of them. I don't remember how many times Angel and I kissed as I asked her to please reconsider and come with me. I never said good-bye to Laoni. As I walked down the path to the street bundled against the cold, I knew I would never see them again. Then I heard her little voice in my head... or was it?

"Thank you for the hot chocolate, Papa Steven, thank you."

Once again, the wind of my aloneness blew through my heart, and the cold dried my tears. I carried the cumbersome weight of another painful goodbye, my knapsack, and the same ten dollars that I had entered Vancouver with three years earlier in the winter of 1979.

In a daze, I zig-zagged my way through the streets of the city one last time back toward the highway, stuck out my thumb, and waited for a ride. I was numb with the familiar feelings of isolation, loss, and anger. I wanted to plan a way to keep Billy away from them. Would he listen to reason? Do I hurt him? Do I kill him? I haven't the money or means to bribe him. All spelled violence and trouble, and I was done with both. I cried so long and so hard over this realization that I lost my bearings, sitting down in the cold by the side of the road, lost in victimhood, heartbroken. I was tired of living. Maybe I'll just step in front of the next truck that rolls by.

FARTHER NORTH
SPRING, 1979

Three days later I had made it all the way to the town of Golden, off Highway 99. I missed Angel and Laoni no less than the day I turned and walked away, but I had become balanced and had climbed out of the sickening fog of loss, assessing what I had and what was next. The old, "screw this, I'm outta here" topography of thought took hold of me once again as I rooted out the seeds of regret, not wanting to stumble past what would be next. Instead, getting ready for whatever it was that was about to happen. Life once again was the winning ticket. I started looking for shelter and a place to gather myself.

The youth hostels of the late 1970s that grew along the back roads of northwestern Canada were infrequent and most times full. Bunk Beds in dorm-type rooms held the lumpy and stained memories of the bodies that had rested on them before me. Other men, other souls, on their way to nowhere in particular. Why else would they have ended up in a place as remote as this?

Long tables with benches in small dining halls, thick, hot potato soup in aluminum bowls, warm bread, and dairy cream butter from a local farm. Tall cups of buttermilk, black coffee and week-old bananas. Topical conversation with named and nameless men about nothing at all and everything that mattered. This was life on the road, filled with its rapture and romance. Wrought with the kind of loneliness that always left you wanting. As I slept on the second night, I dreamed of Angel. Her hands on my body and her hair across my face as she moved on top of me as we made love. Why was she kicking me? What was she doing? My mind's eye still in her presence as I surfaced, the kicking confirmed the existence of the waking world around me.

Peter was a bear of a man. He was the owner of the hostel and ran a clean, safe, and warm place for those of us who lived on the road. His boot came down on the metal frame of the bed in a weird, syncopated rhythm.

"Hey, you, get up. Do you need work? Are you looking to make some money? There is a school bus out back taking people farther north for farm work."

Drawing my first waking breath, not knowing what he was saying, I replied, "I'm in."

"Grab what gear you have. There's hot coffee and day-old doughnuts in the back of the bus. What's your name?"

"Steven."

"Well, Steven, it pays forty bucks a week plus room and board."

"Thank you, sir."

Please, kid, call me Pete. And you're welcome, but don't thank me yet. It's not easy work and not for everyone. Let's go, kid – hustle, that bus won't wait for you. When it's full, it will leave."

I spent the next four months cleaning stalls, feeding goats, horses, and cattle, doing dishes in the mess hall and sleeping and eating with all the other hired help. I recognized some of the guys from Pete's hostel. We kept each other company, evenings at the local bar. Drinking Labatt Beer and putting money in the jukebox, talking shit, and looking at the asses of the girls that walked by, hoping their boyfriends wouldn't catch us staring. The work was steady and paid well, with room and board. Most of us had no homes to go back to, so we worked right through the holidays. One of the farmers we worked for actually gave us a cooked turkey for Thanksgiving. Six of us spent Christmas and New Year's in the barracks sitting around a potbelly stove, playing cards, smoking bad weed, and drinking cheap liquor. Winter slowly made its departure. I decided to take my cue from Mother Nature and hit the road as the weather improved.

It had been four long years; I was a different man. The road had been brutal and beautiful. I'd seen much. Experiencing love and home for the first time in a long time with Angel and Laoni. Love, so concrete. Unmovable until it crumbles into dust and falls through your fingers, soon revealing its silent partner, heartbreak. Through death, departure, the depravity of abuse, or mistrust, heartbreak will take you to task for letting down your guard. Following you around to make sure you are wallowing in it up to your ears.

Still carrying baggage I had no use for any longer, I once again found myself by myself. The time had come to really go home. To come back from this long journey from childhood, which had taken me around the world and left me on my own for the past decade. I was tired of running around. I felt a need in me to sink my road weary roots and make a real life for myself. I knew that there was someone and something more permanent back home. I packed my stuff, collected my pay and turned east, heading to New York.

TIMID THE DOG
FALL, 1979

I saw the thick, black columns of smoke puncturing the air first and intuitively knew from the smell and speed with which the smoke was rising that it was tires burning. As I got closer, it was the tires of a navy blue, late model Benz that lay on its back in the middle of the road, the roof almost completely crushed, except for a small part of the back seat. An assortment of emergency service vehicles was parked helter-skelter, blocking the county road in both directions, flashers on. The driver, an old man, wasn't wearing a seatbelt. He was thrown through the windshield of his car when he tried to avoid hitting a moose. The dead moose lay in the middle of the road. The driver's broken body lay amongst the shattered glass, leaves, dirt ,and debris of his death, some twenty feet from the wreck, covered in a grey flannel blanket, now starting to sport red dots from the broken corpse that lay under it. Carnage and the smell of burning rubber were viscerally disturbing to me, instantly triggering the instinctual fight or flight. Survive and thrive or stay, risk fate, and hope to come away unscathed for the most part. How far away from civilization did I have to get to avoid seeing needless death. It seemed to follow me the hell around, at times tricking me into believing I wouldn't have to endure anymore of its horrors.

A large group of determined EMS workers stood around the car, pointing and talking in an agitated and frustrated manner. A gaggle of drivers who had stepped out of their cars because the road was now blocked had moved closer for a better look. Everyone seemed to be shaking their heads surrounding the overturned vehicle in a kind of horseshoe. Closer to the wreck was a group of firefighters putting out the fire with sand and water, staring intently into the wreck, looking at something inside. I could hear parts of their conversation, "What can we do? The damn animal is stuck way in the back under all that debris."

"Shoot the unfortunate thing. Its back is probably broken anyway. Look how it's sitting, all that blood. Why let it suffer?"

The town of Golden, British Columbia, had been good to me. I was leaving town with two hundred and twenty dollars, a really warm secondhand sweater, and hat that I had purchased from the local Salvation Army with some of my earnings.

I moved even closer to get a better look. Instinctually, knowing it was a mistake. I walked as close as I could to the overturned car and looked inside. I peered in through the ripples of heat and smoke. There was a huge dog in the back seat, whimpering in fear, and most likely pain.

Observe, assess, plan, execute.

"Okay, I've got this. I've been through worse." Everyone stopped what they were doing and looked at me. Why do my decisions at times invoke that WTF look on people's faces? Even to this day? Looking at their expressions, it reminded me of the pigeon-men on the roof of the tenements long ago as they watched me jump the uneven roofs, from building to building.

The sheriff lowered his rifle, visibly relieved that he didn't need to shoot a dog. I handed my knapsack, new second hand sweater, and hat to the sheriff. Wearing a cold wet grey blanket around my shoulders and a helmet that the firemen gave me, and a pair of work gloves someone else had handed me, I made my way into the wreck through a sea of broken glass, twisted metal, and shredded upholstery. My eyes were watering from the smoke. I felt the heat from the burning vehicle above me and the coolness of the water they were spraying coming down on my head and body, soaking the blanket even more. Amazingly, chilling me against the heat. I also felt my knees and hands starting to bleed from the shards of glass and metal, too small to be stopped by worn-out jeans and work gloves.

It was the biggest dog I had ever seen. It had deeply intelligent, huge golden-brown eyes that were now totally fixed on me. The amazing creature before me instinctively, in a flash, knew that I was there to save it. It started whining and softly stamping its paws in anticipation and relief. Its coat was a thick brown, silvery mane. The density of its coat must have saved it from getting any more injured than it already was. It had large cuts on its paws and stomach, small pieces of glass on its snout, and it looked like one of its front legs was sticking out in the wrong direction. I crawled closer, inching toward the animal and holding my breath, trying to keep the wet towel over my nose and mouth. Looking at the blood pooling below the dog's body as the cuts bled unchecked, I moved still closer, my stomach in knots of fear. I could hear the dog breathing; it was rapid and raspy.

"I'm coming, big guy, almost there."

The next second, he was in my arms. He had somehow gathered enough strength and courage to make his move. He wasn't stuck, and his back was definitely not broken. Scared to move through all the glass and smoke. He had pushed himself as far back from the heat and debris as he could. Now I was the one who was scared. There was no way to move back, only forward. The heat had died down, and people were screaming that the fire was out and to keep moving across to the other side and they would help us out of the wreck. By a sheer collective will to survive, we crawled out of that car together, each one almost pushing and pulling the other one along, propelling us out the other side into waiting arms of the EMS and police. I was covered in the dog's blood and my own. The dog's solid weight against my body as he relaxed into my arms was a sign. It was going to be okay. His kisses on my cheeks and face said it all. His breath and tongue were surprisingly cool and wet. Then he looked at me with those eyes of his and said, "I know what you did. Thank you."

Kissing him gently on his head and crying my eyes out, I whispered, "You're welcome, big guy, my pleasure..."

The primal bond between man and dog instantaneously anchored itself deep in my heart, in my being, making my eyes water even more. Knowing it was now safe, the dog collapsed in my arms and started to whine from its pain as the shock of its experience started to wear off. My knees and elbows were cut and bleeding. I shook and cried as they loaded us both into the ambulance.

The whole ordeal of crawling in and out of the burning car, bringing me and my furry survivor back to safety, had lasted only five minutes. The volunteer firemen wrapped us both in blankets. They lovingly started to clean the dog's cuts. Another EMT helped me clean myself up, as well.

Everyone, including me, were shaking their heads, not believing what just happened. Shouts of "Nice work, man," and spattered applause punctured the air, still smelling of burning rubber and tragedy. Most of my cuts were superficial and just needed cleaning, light bandaging, and removing some of the glass and debris from my knees I had crawled through. The dog and I never took our eyes off each other. I stayed close, always with one hand on his back or head, kissing him, letting him know it was going to be okay and that I was there, that he was safe. A second ambulance arrived and took the dead man to the mortuary. A flatbed truck took his dead car to a local dump.

Doc Simon's office, Goldin's only animal doctor; I sat there for two hours while he and his staff cleaned, X-rayed and then stitched the unfortunate animal together, splinting his broken front right foot. When Doc was done, I lifted my sixty-five pound friend into my arms and carried him out into the back of Doc's pick up.

I named him Tim, short for "timid" because he really was a big mush and a magnificent animal. For the next three months, I lived in a cabin on Doc Simon's property for free. My new position was to nurse both Tim and I back to health and help Doc with cleaning the stalls and cages for his various, pawed patients. The cabin had a small kitchen, a smaller bed, and an outhouse around back. We cooked and warmed our water on a potbelly stove. Both Tim and I healed and licked our wounds together. I cleaned and dressed his cuts and bruises every morning and happily shared a lumpy too small bunk bed every night. I never received a bill for the veterinarian's service and care. Doc said they were even considering what I had done to save Tim's life then heal him back to health. As Tim became stronger and able to walk again, he never left my side, nor I his.

Mr. Harold Fessner, eighty-three years old retired teacher then principal of the local public school. Widower, no children or grandchildren. Just him and his big bear of a dog. They were coming from his sister's place the day the moose crossed the road, ending his life, and placing Tim in mine. Tim ended up staying with Doc Simon in his forever home. The day I left, Doc had to hold Tim back from chasing me down the road.

BOOK FOUR
THE ROAD HOME

A SOFT AND SOLID SPACE
1980

Wanderlust had run its course; I had had enough. Safety, peace of mind. The two are inextricably linked. Both mocking me. Mere illusions. Mirages of reprieve. Triumph and loss rose and fell off the memories of all the roads I had traveled the past ten years. Each promised me their salvation, falling short as I sank into a moat of quicksand of my own making, each time. It surrounded the protective arms of acceptance I so longed for and the idea that this might finally be it.

My quest, and detrimentally my mistake since I left my mother's grip, was to poke around in all the wrong places. Finally stumbling upon what I comically thought was where I belonged. I let it lull me into a sense of security. Harboring the idea that I didn't deserve either its safety or the peace of mind it brought. Convinced that I wasn't good enough, I would intentionally place myself in a situation that could kill me... literally kill me.

I had lived many lives for a young man of twenty-three.

I longed for a soft and solid space to lay my head.

TERRA FIRMA
1980

An autumn morning, during rush hour in late November, I believe. These dates and months are somewhat of a blur. Delivered safe and sound into the waiting arms of New York City's Port Authority. Stepping off the bus, down the escalator, and into the majesty of her gum-spotted pavement, excess humanity, and car exhaust. I took a long inhale, taking it all in. The city welcomed me home like a gear slipping back into the mix of the well-oiled machine. Perfect. I headed downtown on the Sixth Avenue F train to Delancey Street.

I had decided the safest place would be in the arms of my friends at Senior's. Hopefully, there was a place to crash for a while. Not Bobby's old place, until I figured my next move.

The subway was familiar; I slid through its belly like I never left its bowels. It welcomed me back, wrapping me in its electric ironclad memories...

Saturdays with my Grandpa Moe. My best friend. Both of us dressed to the nines, bathed in summer sweat, the sweetness of our moment and the anticipation of our next great adventure on our island of dreams. His smile a beacon in the dark still, even though his light had gone out years ago. The memory of his unconditional love saved me at times when times grew uncontrollably dark and out of control. The seats, now solid plastic, no longer padded and covered in wicker, swaying, cradling me against the conflict going on in my mind as the trains moved closer to downtown. The faces and dress of my fellow New Yorkers had changed quite a bit. It seemed less severe, more fluid. The feeling of urgency to get to where we all had to go was still very present.

The familiar cornices and roofs of the tenement buildings moved themselves into view as I ascended the steps of the subway at the corners of Essex and Delancey, equating my ascension from the subway to climbing out of a grave. For the third time in my life, I had come here looking for salvation and shelter from the storm. I had come back this second time for what? Momentarily I paused, shaking my head, chasing the question back into hiding, putting it back in its place for later inspection.

Essex Street Market still sending its perfumed endorsement of fresh and rotting things. Hearing the multitude of languages, it felt good to be home. The overwhelming panoramic filth, misfortune, and gloom that I, as a scared and abused thirteen-year-old, felt from this place the first time I was here now seemed docile, scripted.

I am twenty-three. Fully upright. Unafraid of everything but myself. This suffocating place that taught me how to breathe. This place I had forced myself upon so violently. This was still my turf. Its form, sound, color, and mass of human flesh, overwhelming in the limited confines of its invisible borders, was still intact. I stood there, the midday sunlight warming my face in the heated familiarity of knowing in that moment, with full confidence, who I was. I am finally my own man. A man standing at street level.

I danced across Delancey Street. Between cars, trucks, buses and push carts and masses of people, I headed west, weaving my way toward Senior's place on Mott Street, seven blocks away. I hadn't seen that much concrete or people in one place in a long time. My jungle of concrete, manipulation, and garbage had not lost its magic; the cracks in its veneer in plain view were still easy to spot.

I pushed through the door of Senior's club with authority, like it had been hours not years since I crossed its threshold. I knew I didn't look like the same kid that had walked through those same doors, going the opposite way, five extraordinarily long, years before. As my hair grew longer, it began to curl, resting on my shoulders. Road weary, intelligent eyes that spoke of nothing until asked, three days of growth on my face, sneakers, and a beat-up army jacket, I looked like a dangerous situation.

Walking through the front door, they all freaked out. I should have known better. Everyone jumped up, spilling drinks and food all over themselves, each other, the floor and tables, hands on their weapons all pointing at me. Time always slows down to slow-mo in times like these, giving those of us within the trigger hairs to do or say something.

"Where is my bat? You assholes said you'd hold it for me." They stopped dead, looking from me to Senior, then back at me again. Tony was the first to recognize me. Still holding his piece, he ran over and lifted me off the ground. Kissing my cheek and telling everyone else it was me. Out of the corner of my eye I saw Senior, his smiling eyes burned into mine. Both Jerry and Tony were hugging me, asking me questions, getting me a beer and telling me to sit down. Senior stood up after some minutes; Tony and Jerry backed off, and I stepped into Senior's safe, strong embrace.

"Welcome home, kid. I knew you'd come back. Now, give this fuck his bat back so we can all have a drink, capiche?"

I had been around the world, and it showed. I wasn't the kid carrying a bat under his denim jacket anymore, selling nickel bags of weed and stolen fish. I had the stance and distant stare of someone who might have seen a bit too much in too short a period of time. Three beers and numerous joints later, I told them everything, end to end. Even my time overseas, leaving out as much detail as I could. The cast of characters over the past years had been eclectic to say the least. Junior had kept my flat on Eldridge Street, paying the rent to the new landlord and using my space as a kind of office/private space. Senior still had the club. Now painted white on the outside with a huge Italian and American flag on either side of the entrance.

MARCH, 1982

I ended up settling in a small apartment above Senior's club. We picked up where we had left off and went about the business of taking care of business for Senior. Two years passed by in a blur. Things on the street had changed. There was too much heroin out there. This was a different type of heroin. It was toxic. Piles of people in alleyways and slumped on ours stoops. Dirty needles and empty dime bags with symbols of the dealers who sold their individual death littered the streets. There was no way to control it or the humanity that gravitated here. Unstable lines of junkies threading their way through Sarah Roosevelt Park every day waiting for their dealers to arrive, dressed in suits and rags, sneakers and Ferragamos. The Ferragamos, holding hundred-dollar bills, the sneakers carrying dirty wads of singles and fives in their piss-stained clothing. Moms strung out with baby carriages giving blow jobs out in the open for enough change to get a fix. Fucked up people of all shapes and sizes standing on a line to die. The cops drove by like the line was for the Good Humor Ice Cream truck on a hot August day. Instead of stopping and arresting the dealers, they aggressively picked on everyone else for selling dime bags of weed and drinking open bottles or cans of beer on our stoops. They made our lives more difficult and more expensive, having to pay them more or supply them with weed, free pussy, or a winning number just to keep them off our backs. We all knew that the supply was coming from a much greater source. Other families that didn't give a shit about anything but money and power. This infuriated Senior. As much as he complained it was out of his hands. He got very well compensated. The money seemed to flow in from everywhere. Even if it was made from the death and misery of others, it totaled into the tens of thousands of dollars annually.

It seemed to us that for every dead junkie pulled off the street, two would take his or her place. It was so much worse and more pervasive than when I had moved down here in 1968 and watched as my junkie cousin was beaten to death for selling bad dope. Compared to the debauchery and violence now, it seemed mundane.

Senior kept us mostly away from the carnage. We spent most of the time keeping the junkies and dealers away from us and the places we did our thing, selling weed, loaning money, running numbers and directing people across the Bowery to illegal card games in Mr. Lee's Chinatown. The opium dens had long since closed, now that there was a better way to get high.

There was an element of newness and youth that seemed to color and energize this new and expanding landscape we called our home. They seemed to be fighting for the same space the drug users were using. These young people had red and green hair, cut, gelled, and spiked into sometimes seemingly impossible configurations. Leaving me and the guys wondering how they slept at night without ripping the sheets on their beds. There was a sense of rebellion and freedom to choose that attracted me to this new movement. The Lower East Side was humming with the sounds of amazing rock and roll. I spent countless hours in CBGB. Sometimes sitting tables away from Allen Ginsberg and other anti-folk heroes and beat poets, listening to the Ramones, Patti Smith, and Tom Waits. I saw the Police and the Talking Heads.

JULY 4TH, 1982

I woke up that day to the persistent hum of my bedroom air conditioner and the muffled pops of firecrackers on the street below through the closed window. The A/C unit was a gift from a friend who said it fell off the back of a truck. It was an amazing machine to have, growing up in the heat of the past summers.

I lay there in the cool heat of my darkened room, realizing it would be my twenty-sixth year on this ridiculous planet next month. It was time, once again, to move on and find a life and a life partner. A normal, more sustainable life, away from the harsh and manipulative world I had called home for most of my youth. I laid back and closed my eyes, feeling the cool air wash over me, letting my mind do its thing.

I still had a good sum of money in "Senior's bank" from my time overseas that I hadn't touched. There was no need. My pocket was always lined with twenty-dollar bills from all the carrying on and business I did on the streets. Tony, Jerry, and Senior were always within view. We fell back into our friendship without a second thought. We were all men. All kings. Our stoops were replaced by square blocks. We have people in places who we trusted, streetwise, with resumes only reputation and longevity can produce. Unmatched. More muscle and less hustle to get things done. I never raise my voice or hands to anyone anymore. None of us had to. There is no need. I received more of everything and anything I would ever need . . . and never asked how it was acquired. Senior got his cut, we made a shitload of money and never paid for anything. Most days we would sit at our table at the back of Dominic's eating pizza and warm zeppole covered in fresh powdered sugar, washed down with Diet Cokes and gin mixed in paper Dixie cups. Sending and receiving our "employees" about their business.

Again, that itch. That change in the atmosphere that always roused my static complacency. I got out of bed and took a really hot shower. It came clear through all the steam that I knew if I put myself out there, instead of succumbing to the laziness and ease of the Lower East Side life, I'd find what I was looking for.

Two hours later, wearing my last clean white T-shirt, a pair of jeans, and work boots, I said good-bye to my friends for what, unknowingly, would actually be the final time some of us would share the same air. No one believed me and didn't pay much attention when I said I was leaving. Not looking back, I walked through the doors of Senior's club. I boarded the uptown D train. With all my cash, a knapsack full of relics and meaningless crap from my past, and hair down to my waist held back in a ponytail. I changed to the F train on 34th Street across the platform for no apparent reason, sat down, and fell asleep.

I turned my back and walked away for the last time in that summer of 1983 from a place that will always be a part of who I am, of what I am, of the kind of man I am to others. Both good and bad.

I didn't step foot back inside Senior's club on Mott Street until 2019 when Jerry called me, asked me about the book I had started writing, never saying how he knew about it or even how he knew where to get in touch with me. Without missing a beat, I took the subway downtown and read it to him for his approval and his input. He was the last man standing. Still a big dude but more sedated, gray. Senior had died of cancer in 2002, leaving the club to Jerry. Tony was just getting out of prison after a ten year vacation upstate for armed robbery and aggravated assault... using a bat.

THE GIRL ON THE E TRAIN
1984

I woke up sometime later on Continental Boulevard in Queens. I was completely disoriented. I staggered off the train with my belongings and walked up the steps to the crossover heading west and took my place on the platform with everyone else heading to Manhattan.

Craning my neck to see if a train was coming, my eyes were drawn to the most beautiful woman I had ever seen, about my age, guarding two suitcases of her own, looking a bit determined and completely in charge of her surroundings. It seemed at first glance that we were carrying our lives and belonging to new destinations. Running from one thing and hoping to run into the arms of something better. I was drawn to her. Magically, there seemed to be a light that cast its protective aura all around her. Did she notice me walking toward her? Did I look as disheveled as I felt? Frantically thinking of what to say. I said hello . . .

Her name was Gail. I was smitten. We started talking, took the train to Grand Central, found a coffee shop, kept talking, fell in love, moved in together months later, and never looked back. She was open, funny, honest, full of heart, and drop-dead gorgeous. We were married in a brownstone in the West Village two years later on September 15, 1986.

West Village, Jane Street. My marriage to Gail. Our wedding, 1986. True story: the photographer was so high on weed, this was the only photo that came out.

A LIFE GIVEN, A LIFE TAKEN

SEPTEMBER, 1988

We both wanted a child. When it was the right time we tried, then tried again, and again, and again for two years. After two miscarriages, the absolute heartbreak and searing pain of the stillbirth of another little boy, Gail almost made it to full term. Then at seven months, her water broke almost killing our unborn son.

On September 18, 1988, our boy Zackary Jordan Borodkin was born at twenty-five weeks. Months too early, he was cut out and taken from his mom's womb, delivered into our world kicking and screaming, weighing in at just under three pounds. He was a sick little boy. Gail also became septic and spent weeks in the hospital on the same floor as Zack, being treated with extremely aggressive antibiotics to save her life. For days after Gail's arrival at the hospital and Zack's arrival into this world, it was touch and go for both of them. Sleepless nights at the hospital. A parade of friends and family bringing hot coffee, sandwiches, and support. After a short but scary twenty-four hours, Gail responded well to her medication and came around very quickly once the antibiotics took hold in her system.

Zack, however, lived in the hospital for the next three months. His small, sickly, yellow, doll-like body strapped, taped and pinned to numerous I.V lines, monitors, and machines, staying alive by the grace of God and the amazing twenty-four-hour care of his doctors and nurses in the neonatal intensive care unit at Lenox Hill Hospital on East 68th Street. Zack's body was not yet ready for this world or its atmosphere, making it exceedingly hard on him the first weeks on this earth. He was so premature that every time his heart took a beat and the blood pumped up through his brain, it would cause his head to bleed. He was also on an experimental drug at the time that helped seal up certain parts of his tiny heart that weren't quite ready yet. Yet, through all these trials, we watched him evolve, adapting to his world around him. It seemed logical to us that he was ready to be a part of it. He fought hard, gaining little bits of strength and weight every day. I went to work from the hospital, Gail recovered and spent her days at his side with her mother, Margaret, marveling and praying over the newest family member.

Three months later on December 6th, as he finally tipped the scales at five pounds, he was ready to go home. Zack's doctor and nurse guided us into a small low-lit room. As we entered, Gail and I immediately felt the emotion that filled the small space. The pain and shock, sadness, and loss permeated everything.

The windowless little room was furnished in the nondescript aesthetic that only a hospital could achieve. A box of tissues and empty coffee cups scattered across the side table and coffee table, chairs pulled close to each other seemly huddled, waiting for the next set of occupants to come unburden their grief and uncomfortable conversations and leave. Scarred linoleum floors, glossy generic brochures with titles about breast or bottle, postnatal depression, and suggesting ways to cope while grieving for a premature baby. Hope and survival faded as they led us away from the crowd of parents and family to speak in private. The sick, clean smell of cleanser and grief. The fine lines of dust around the table lamps, that cast their dark and threatening shadows in the corners the light didn't want to reach. We were directed to sit down on dark navy blue vinyl seats. They sighed and hissed in protest as the air ran out of them from the weight of our exhaustion. We held on to each other, already badly bruised emotionally from all we had been through, all that Gail and our sick little boy had been through.

The doctor began to tell us that due to an extremely early birth and resulting complications during his fight to survive, that our darling son Zack would be physically and mentally challenged. That he would live an extremely limited life due to a congenital heart condition and lung disease. If he did manage to survive, he would need perpetual care for the rest of his remaining life. Gail collapsed onto my shoulder in deep heaving sobs, I collapsed into myself, holding my wife and holding back my own tears. My vision became telescoped as if the room was growing away from me. Was this my fault? Was my son paying for the many sins of his father? Did God think I wasn't worthy of being a father? I faded from the reality of what we had just been told. I gently helped Gail lift herself up as we rose off our chairs. We walked down the hall and spent the next part of the day simply holding hands, standing by his bed, crying, praying, and gazing at this beautiful little miracle, our son, feeling helpless and confused. We went home to try to get a good night's sleep. We would figure out our next move in the morning,

The following day Gail went back to Lenox Hill Hospital as she had done for the past twelve weeks with her mother to spend the day at our baby boy's bedside. I took the train out to see my father in Queens at his repair shop. We cried like babies in each other's arms as I explained the situation. As we both wiped our eyes, I told him what I planned to do.

"I'm not going to let this little soul suffer anymore or place this burden on Gail and myself, Dad. I'm going to pull the plug and stand by the bed till he stops breathing. I already love him more than I can say, and my son will not lead a short, painful, isolated life."

My father became apoplectic, shaken to the core by what I had just shared with him. He screamed at me, calling me a murderer, a cold young man who had seen too much to feel anything for anyone but himself. I kept my mouth closed and let my father react then kissed him on his now hot and flushed forehead and walked away, shaking, out of his office, telling him I loved him. Everyone in the shop had heard what we shouted at each other…I walked back to the subway and headed to the hospital.

I arrived at Lenox Hill Hospital on Lexington Avenue and 68th Street soon after my father, who had driven his car. He had somehow gotten there at the same time, believing that I was going to carry out my plan. He cut me off in the lobby as we passed through the revolving doors, not knowing that by the time I arrived at the hospital I'd reconsidered going through with this terribly self-destructive plan. This was my son, my boy, my flesh and blood—the realization hit me harder than any bat ever could. The love I felt for him had been woven into me long before he was born, coursing through my veins and destined to last forever.

"Stevie, kiddo, stop and think, please. I know how you must feel. This is your son, my grandson. No matter what you feel, you must give life a chance. I won't let you harm him." I opened my mouth to tell him that he didn't know how I felt, and that I had utterly changed my mind. Then, in a deep Scottish lilt, we heard, "Howard Borodkin, Steven? What on earth?"

A cosmic bilateral shift had occurred, pulling the two of us and this voice in and out of the surrounding reality just enough to pause in stupefied recognition. These few moments I remember vividly. "Doctor Manners? Doctor Sydney Manners?" my father asked in disbelief, the name sounding alien, kind off ridiculous. Catching our breath, letting it all sink in, we hugged and exchanged strained pleasantries, then found a corner in the lobby where we laid out our story as cohesively as we could, considering that we were explaining it to a man we had not seen in nearly twenty years.

Incredibly, this very doctor, who had delivered and then cared for me as a child, a man neither of us had seen in decades, had just stepped through the elevator door of a random hospital and put out the fire. What were the odds of ever seeing this man again, and under these circumstances?

Three floors above and half a hallway down from the elevator, seemly another world away, both Gail and her wonderful mother, Margaret, while praying over Zack, had gone through their own divine encounter. They stood for hours, praying over our son, his little body housed in an oxygen tent of tubes and wires. Mother and daughter's hands clasped together in love and faith. Praying over and over again. Eyes closed, thanking the Lord for His grace and forgiveness to heal this beautiful little soul, our son, Zack. Just as they had done for all these days, weeks, and months.

Both mother and daughter saw it and felt it. As they asked God over and over for Zack to survive, it seemed the Almighty had heard enough and had picked up the phone. Sending a message through them of love and healing so strongly it changed everything forever for our family. There was a distant tinge of ozone and electricity in the room, all happening as my father, Dr. Manners, and I walked into Zack's room, still feeling hung over from the rush of adrenaline and our unexpected shock moments earlier. Both of these dreamlike events joined together. Each of these circumstances had contributed to creating a third experience. A kind of one plus one equals three. For the first time since his birth, Zack moved his hands and feet. Opening his eyes with recognition and seeing his family for the first time. We were humbled and smitten with deep faith and belief for this series of serendipitous events. I kept going back to the feeling that passed through me when I was baptized by Pastor Mike a lifetime ago in the cold waters of Washington state.

Things changed rapidly after that day. Zack became stronger; he started to eat and react to the medication he was given. Three weeks later, he had gained enough weight for us to take him home. Dr. Manners came to see him every day before we left the hospital.

We took Zack home in a rented limo with our dear friend and photographer Maurice videotaping the whole journey. I remember the radio announcing that Roy Orbison had died that day as we settled into the back of the car. One life taken, one life given.

My warrior son. Zack was born with Cerebral Palsy and went

through so many different surgeries and medical procedures over the following years. Both major and minor. Each time going through it all with God's grace and patience. Gail became Zack's advocate, and to support them, I opened my own service-based company, installing motorized shades and draperies for the interior design industry. During the '90s and right through September 11th, we were one of the largest companies of our kind. Design Resource Services, or DRS as we were most commonly known. We did well over a million dollars a year for a decade. I started that company with eighty-nine dollars and someone else's tools. Never looking back, always there for my family.

As Zack's full-time advocate, Gail tirelessly researched and secured medical care from some of New York's top doctors. Driven by unwavering determination and faith in Zack's potential, she also succeeded in placing him in schools best suited to provide him with the highest quality education.

Zach is just three months old. Taken at my Aunt Sue and Uncle Harold's home on Long Island, 1988.

Queens, New York (my grandparents' house). Gail took this with our Polaroid. I was fiercely protective of my boy. To this day, I am the same way. He is the deepest part of my joy.

North South Lake, Upstate New York, 1992, camping. Gail took this photo with our Polaroid.

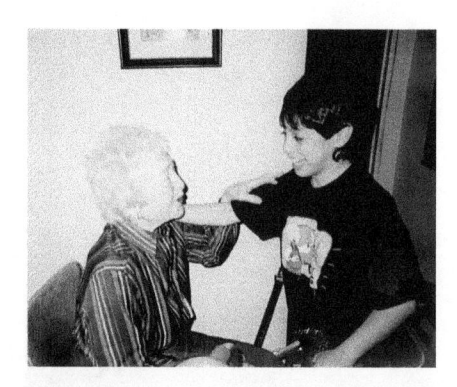

Queens, New York, 1995. Zack and his great grandmother (my dad's mother, my grandma Mina). She is in her late nineties.

Zack went on to lead a normal life, with friends, family, and the world at his feet. He finished college and went on to graduate school and is now employed with a non-profit as an advocate for the disabled and is thinking about running for some public office. He grew up with more aunts and uncles than you can shake a fist at. Each one of our friends showered him with love and support, still to this day.

Without exception, I thank the universe for my son, Zack, his existence, and his light each day. As Gail and I, with the help of God and love of so many others, contributed and saved his life, he gave all of ours unconditional, continuing joy. Through all his pain, Zack never stopped smiling, growing, and asking for more, and by example, showing us that it can be done. That being complete is not all about being physical but, at times, a delicate balance of the emotional, physical, and the cerebral. I would not be the man I am today if not for the love of his amazing mother and the unconditional love that came to the three of us through the idea of simply being grateful for what we had. I know that God touched my son that day in the hospital after his birth. The love and blessings of that day still surround us. We all feel its power in the love that fills our lives. His childhood, although most times challenging and painful, was as bright and beautiful as we could make it. My family, and all who he touched, embraced my son. I embraced all of my family...

leaving my mother at full arm's length. We three, family, unstoppable and unshakable in our collective journey, broke the chain that had tethered my family to dysfunctional levels for decades through the disability of my son. It has taken a lifetime to sit and write these words, these memories, raw and poetic. Chaos in Christmas wrapping at times. A sweet reminder that love and redemption are real.

Here's to you, Zack. You are the beat of my heart. You are the heat in the flame of our future. You continue to make me proud. The sins of the father have been placed in a box and buried.

Gail and Zach, Graduation Day, Binghamton University, 2016.

Harlem, Summer 2018.

A LIFE GIVEN, A LIFE TAKEN • 199

Sag Harbor, New York, 2020.

Flight to Los Angeles, 2024.

AFTERWORD

I do not consider myself a writer in the truest sense of its meaning, although I have been told differently by those that have read some of my jottings. Do all writers talk as much as I do?

I mean, if I am of that ilk, are we all this loquacious?

The genesis of the previous pages you've just ingested and hopefully enjoyed, are a metamorphosis, from my spoken word to my written word. Prompted by my dear friend Carlton, a retired science professor, and my amazing life partner Deb, after hearing me tell these stories of my life, to write them all down.

These "written words" took seven hundred and thirty drafts, a lot of research and thought, all of ten years, the patience of my family, then, finally, the open heart, intelligence, and hard work of my first editor, then finally an amazing publisher and her team. Having the agency for retrospect and introspection in writing this memoir has been cathartic, but generally, acutely haunting.

Writing any book, or type of construct of self-expression (because that is what the written word is), always places my feet in two different worlds. One foot in this realm and one in the reality of what I am writing at the time. Street Level had me utterly submerged in my past.

A memoir could be a journal of the times in your life you feel noteworthy, or not worthy of, but of mentioning. Life changing, knowingly different from other people around you. In a way, you are acknowledging the art of storytelling, mingled with (in my situation) revelation to those closest to you, of the why, who, and how of the man I am and the person they know, and thought they really knew.

This narrative will, for some, serve as the mislaid segments of a jigsaw puzzle, unlocatable, forgotten for years under the davenport, only when discovered making you assemble the puzzle again to its fullest the way it should have been seen to begin with. Finally understanding, contemplating it now in its fullness, its depth, its beauty, and its flaws.

I had a wonderful man in my life for many, many years, my therapist, Mark. He knew I was a different kind of man, not better or worse comparatively. Through years of deep, difficult, reflective, and at times joyful work, he showed me what I interpreted as the fact that I own an anomalous, sometimes searching passion to live, to survive. He once told me that I was blessed to be an odd and artistic self-taught intelligent man, full of heart and humor. It was one of the kindest and most observant things anyone has ever said to me. He passed away in 2021.

Thank you to all who read and shared in my journey. Each of us have our own trials and journeys. There is no real goal, only the next step toward finding ourselves. Gathering close to us things nonmaterial we can hold close to our hearts. Hopefully, you came away with the feeling of simply enjoying a great read. Possibly you saw something of yourself, of your childhood, your family. Maybe you saw a reflection of your own abuse in mine. If you did, I know, I'm sorry. You are not alone. There are a lot of us. I know, dear ones, that each of us own some odd and wonderful thing that makes us all beautiful and flawed works of art.

"Sing so loud that the devil can hear you, and heaven knows your name."

Steve

ABOUT THE AUTHOR

Steve has spent most of his adult life crafting poetry, prose, and short pieces, though he never quite saw it as "the real thing." Now, this book and the stories within it stand as his true biography. A published poet and passionate writer, musician, animal activist and cancer survivor, Steve makes his home on the East End of Long Island with his life partner, Debra, and their two beloved dogs.

Writing more than ever these days, Steve reflects, "At seventy, I've had many lives with many stories—then again, haven't we all?" He is currently working on his second book, continuing his journey of self expression and storytelling.